Madonna King is an award-winning journalist, compère and author. She has had 25 years' experience in the media, covering everything from business to politics, across newspapers, radio and television. She has publicly interviewed dozens of corporate CEOs for the Australian Institute of Company Directors' Leaders' Edge Lunch Series and is the author of five books including *Hockey: Not Your Average Joe*; *Ian Frazer: the man who saved a million lives* and, with Cindy Wockner, *One-Way Ticket: the Untold Story of the Bali 9*. For more information, visit www.madonnaking.com.au

MADONNA KING

THINK SMART
RUN HARD

Lessons in business leadership
from **Maxine Horne**

XOUM PUBLISHING

Sydney

All proceeds from the sale of this book will be donated to Act for Kids, an Australian charity providing free therapy and support services to children and families who have experienced, or are at risk of child abuse and neglect.

First published by Xoum**Custom** in 2016

Xoum Publishing
PO Box Q324, QVB Post Office,
NSW 1230, Australia
www.xoum.com.au

ISBN 978-1-921134-74-6 (print)
ISBN 978-1-921134-75-3 (digital)

All rights reserved. Without limiting the rights under copyright below, no part of this publication shall be reproduced, stored in or introduced into a retrieval system, or transmitted in any form or by any means (electronic, mechanical, photocopying, recording or otherwise), without the prior permission of both the copyright holders and the publisher.

The moral right of the author has been asserted.

Text copyright © Madonna King 2016
Cover photograph copyright © Justine Walpole 2016
Illustrations copyright © Dan Boermans 2016
Cover and internal design and typesetting copyright © Xoum Publishing 2016

Cataloguing-in-publication data is available from the National Library of Australia

Cover design by Xou Creative, www.xou.com.au
Printed and bound in Australia by McPherson's Printing Group

Papers used by Xoum Publishing are natural, recyclable products made from wood grown in sustainable forests. The manufacturing processes conform to the environmental regulations of the country of origin.

Contents

Preface	vii
Smart Run to Fortune	1
1. Customer is King (or Queen)	29
2. You Don't Know It All	45
3. Strategy Rules, OK	61
4. Stand and Deliver	75
5. Employ for Will Not Skill	89
6. Look After Your Own	103
7. Lead, Don't Just Manage	119
8. Take Your Partners	141
9. Follow the Ant Trail	155
10. Grow Yourself	169
11. Metrics Matter	179
12. Put Value in Values	193
13. Give Diligence its Due	207
14. Put the Cult into Culture	219
15. Look Over the Fence	231
16. Take Care of Yourself	243
17. Think Smart	253
18. Run Hard	267
Chronology	275
Author's Note	281

Preface

Every life and every career has its ups and down. I've been fortunate that leading the businesses that make up the Vita Group has given me more ups than downs. Upon reaching the milestone of the 21st anniversary of founding the company, I felt it was time to share the lessons I've learnt and the experiences I've had – these are the basis of this book.

Business is never simple and the best decision I made was to jump into the mobile communications business at its outset and then find the right partnerships and people who were willing to build the organisation and better serve our customers. I've made mistakes – some of them expensive, but most of them foreseeable with the benefit of experience. It's as important to talk about our mistakes as it is to talk about our triumphs, which is why I asked author Madonna King to help articulate the lessons from my own ride on this roller coaster.

Success is never solo. I've been lucky throughout my career to have come across some amazing leaders who have not only inspired me, but have also taken me under their wing, making me a better person.

Special thanks to Tricia Mittens who started the journey by ignoring the cross against my name and seeing something in me that no-one else did; for helping me see what I was capable of; for driving discipline in me and for not once allowing me to get away with anything. Over the past 10 years Dick Simpson has been a great mentor and has provided much guidance (sometimes uninvited). He taught me that the teacher can only teach when the student's ready to learn and that the very thing that makes you successful can destroy you – if you don't control it.

I'd like to acknowledge and thank my Vita Peeps, both past and present, some of whom have become very dear friends. They have all put their heart and soul into this business and by doing so when their time has come, have left with more skills than they arrived with. They have all made their mark on the Vita Group. Thank you to Darren Gaunt who joined Vita Group (then Fone Zone) in March 1995 at just 18 and made a significant contribution to our growing business. Darren is a very capable and intelligent young man, and I know that leaving Vita Group was the best development step for him to take. Thank you to John Weir, who in those early days helped me stamp the culture into the soul of this organisation. To Wayne Smith, who taught me the importance of strategy, structure, people, systems and processes, thank you for adding that string to my bow. To my current Group Leadership Team, or GLT as we call it, I am so lucky to be surrounded by a group of very authentic, caring and talented people. Thank you for contributing to the vision of making Vita a Great Place To Be! In the team there's Kendra Hammond who was and still is the quiet overachiever – you've had a huge influence on me and this business, you are the 'glue' that keeps us all together and your daily guidance is invaluable. To Bec McLeod, who has the unenviable job of making sure I get my point across and importantly stay on track (which is no mean feat) and who, by the way, has more of a shoe fetish than I do, thank you. To Wendy Dean, who's been my EA but more importantly my friend for over 10 years, and who continues to make me look efficient, keeps me on time, on schedule, has changed more flights than you could possibly count and keeps me out of trouble … well maybe not the last point!

There are two more special Vita Peeps that I'd like to mention, both of whom came with the intention of staying for only six to 12 months. I can happily say that these very gifted individuals are still here sharing their wisdom. They've been instrumental in the success of this business and are great businessmen and outstanding leaders. To Pete Connors and Andrew Leyden, I say thank you for believing in me, for taking the plunge when you had so many other options, for being beside me when the chips were down and for making our vision come true! Now … let's get back to work. 🙂

On a personal note, thank you to my grandparents who looked after me in those early years, instilling my values. To my father, who taught me resilience and that life's meant to be fun; to Susan who at the tender age of 21 took on what was to become an unruly teenager and despite that fact, has always been there for me and is more like the older sister I never had. I know I've challenged you along the way but like all teenagers I came through the other side. Thank you. To Nathan, my personal trainer, who over many, many years has kept my body fit, healthy and strong so that my mind could be too. To my girlfriends (Suzette, the two Bronwyns, Ali, Louise and Bec), thank you for being there through thick and thin; you've helped me retrieve my mojo and I truly thank you for that.

To David McMahon, without you I would not be in Australia, I would not have seized this opportunity and would not have the amazing life that I have today, so thank you for coming on the journey with me and for our two wonderful children.

On that note, I want to dedicate this book to those very children – Jack and Grace – who truly are beautiful inside and out. You make my heart swell every time I see you and to this day that feeling of unconditional love still overwhelms me. To both of you I say …

Think Smart and Run Hard!

Maxine Horne

THINK SMART
RUN HARD

Smart Run to Fortune

'To be successful, you have to have your heart in your business and your business in your heart.' – Thomas J. Watson Sr, former CEO and driving force behind IBM

Maxine Horne's first purchase was five pairs of pristine white socks. Each morning, the 14 year old would stop in the laneway behind her terraced home, out of sight of both her father Malcolm and stepmother Susan, and swap the red socks she was wearing with the unspoiled white pair she'd hidden in her school bag. Then, knowing she looked just like all the other girls funnelling in through the gates of St Martin's in Caerphilly, she'd run the four kilometres to class.

Caerphilly, in South Wales, is at the southern end of the Rhymney Valley and its geography revealed all the clues needed to mark your social standing in the 1970s. Maxine had to run up – not down – the hill that separated the family's modest home from the moneyed homesteads of her friends. It was a daily reminder that good fortune, or more specifically fortune, was not always fair in its distribution. Maxine's friends, wearing the same regulation blouse and skirt, always wore white socks. Never red. Their families didn't spend much time contemplating the sins the local soil waged on the colour white; perhaps they didn't know that scarlet socks hid the dirt and lasted longer. Maxine wanted to be like everyone else. She didn't want to stand out as one of the cash-strapped students, and red socks spelt poor.

'After school I'd change back into the red socks and walk inside,' Maxine, now 52, says. 'I'd wash my white socks, with Dad yelling at me to get out of the bathroom. I just really didn't want people to know we were poor.'

Maxine was born in 1963 in the English town of Ipswich, 100-odd kilometres northeast of London. Her parents Patricia and Malcolm met on a Butlins holiday camp, billed to appeal to those British families who struggled to afford a getaway. A quick courtship led to marriage a couple of months later and a fractious on-again–off-again relationship that lasted years. From the age of two, Maxine passed between the homes of her mother, and her father's parents George and Rose Horne. Her sister Michelle, born six years later, was predominantly raised by her mother. Eventually, Maxine remained with her grandparents while her father, a gas fitter by trade, worked on the oil rigs in the North Sea off Scotland. That meant he could only visit after long and lonely stints at sea, but Maxine would count down the days until she could be propped up on his shoulders, singing along to 'Yellow Submarine'. Her mother Patricia lived locally, attempting each day to keep her head above the poverty line.

Maxine chooses her words carefully. 'It was a bit like Checkpoint Charlie,' she says, referring to the crossing point between East and West Berlin during the Cold War. 'I felt like a pawn the whole time.'

Her grandparents George and Rose provided both a home and a sureness for the young Maxine, away from the squabbles of her parents, and many of the lessons they taught her guide her ASX-listed telecommunications business Vita Group Limited today. Rose, a cleaner, would bring home her meagre income, dividing it between various tins hidden at the bottom of her wardrobe. Maxine used to watch her, noticing that she never missed making a contribution to both the tin labelled 'electricity' and the one labelled 'food'. That money, supplemented by the vegetables grown in the couple's garden, ensured there was food on the table each night. Sunday was Maxine's favourite; that's when she'd sit down to a special meal, perhaps even a roast. After dinner, the leftovers would be gathered up and used for the next few lunches and dinners. Cornish pasties and toad-in-the-hole were a constant.

'My grandparents were very frugal,' Maxine says. 'They had to be.' She attributes that lesson – of carving up a pay packet to meet expenses – as the reason she now refuses to pay $2 to withdraw money from a non-bank ATM. 'I'm a saver. I still do what they did with the tins – except I divide my earnings up and put it in different bank accounts.'

Maxine's grandfather George was a local carpenter, and had a little shed at the back of their semi-detached council home. After school, he'd invite Maxine in, handing her a hammer, nails and a spare block of wood, encouraging her to join in.

'I was only young – probably eight or nine – but I remember him sitting there, asking me when I was going to start work.'

Maxine's grandparents, along with her unpropitious upbringing, are no doubt behind the career success she enjoys today, and despite their deaths – within a matter of months of each other in 2002 – she refers back to them regularly to explain the lessons she's learnt and the values her company has adopted. The drive to ensure a healthy bank balance has its impetus in her grandparents never having enough money. The bulging property portfolio Maxine has amassed over time is a reminder that her grandparents had to work hard to keep a roof over her head. Her determination to make lunch for her high school-aged daughter Grace is a daily reminder that she's been able to grant a childhood to her children that providence never afforded her. Her love of travel is born from her grandparents' inability to do the same. (While her grandfather was a signalman in the Eighth Army's North African and Italian campaigns during World War II, her grandmother never left the UK.) Children who witness their parents divorce often boast a steely resolve to succeed where they didn't.

Teenage years

Life changed abruptly at age 11 when Maxine's father Malcolm – now with custody of Maxine and her sister Michelle, then aged six – arrived to take them to live in Caerphilly in South Wales with his new wife Susan. Rose and George were devastated to let go of Maxine, but delighted that their son could now support his own family. That didn't stop Maxine, at least for the next few years, counting down the days until school holidays would herald the long trip back to her grandparents' home. But, as evidence of a child's resilience and ability to adapt to new situations, Maxine and Michelle slipped quickly into their new family life – despite Maxine's reluctance to accept Susan at first.

Maxine was her father's favourite. Malcolm, who became the local gas man, never learnt the money lessons his parents had passed onto Maxine. He found asking for payment for his services difficult and would regularly install central heating or do other odd jobs around the neighbourhood without recompense. That left the family struggling to make ends meet. At one point they were recipients of a government voucher system that offered lunch for Maxine and her sister at school.

Maxine loathed the idea of lining up to be handed food in the same way she loathed her red socks. It drew the sharpest contrast, in her mind, between the haves and the have-nots; between those who would cut it in life, and those who would not; between the in-group, and the out-group. She didn't want anyone knowing she couldn't afford the life many of her peers seemed to take for granted.

'We had tickets and had to queue for lunch at school in a separate area so everyone knew who was on social security and who wasn't,' Maxine says. She refused to do it. Instead, each lunchtime, she would skip past the government-issued lunch line-up and head for the school gates. Once outside, she'd run. And run. This time she'd be running downhill, away from that social status marker which dictated where she was positioned in life to the sanctuary of her home. There, in the kitchen, where it was no-one else's business, she'd make herself a jam sandwich.

Maxine wanted to fit in. To be acknowledged, or recognised, would have been the icing on the cake. This became evident on the sporting field, where second equated to last. Her natural athleticism and the thrice-daily runs to school allowed her to feel the triumph granted by a win. She played hard. In netball, she loved being goal shooter and later centre, at the heart of the action. In squash, she worked so that her one-handed backhand was as powerful as her forehand. But it was in track and field that she learnt a valuable lesson that would stay with her, moulding the way she did business in another country, decades later. Winning required more than mere effort. You needed to *want* the prize, and be prepared to fight for it. You needed to meet the challenge brought on by your competitor. One day, while still in high school, Maxine found herself up against one of her wealthy peers who was used to the winner's dais.

'I remember, to this day, thinking that I was going to try to beat her,' Maxine says now. By the finish line, Maxine had lapped the usual winner, her smile never broader. Her physical education teacher, not knowing why she wasn't on her track team, made a beeline for her.

'Who are you?' the teacher demanded.

'I'm Maxine Horne.'

'Where are your running shoes?'

'I don't have any.'

'Come with me and I'll give you some.' In silence, she walked alongside her teacher to the track and field lost property box. 'Put these on,' the teacher told Maxine, presenting her with a second-hand pair of shoes. 'You're on the track team.'

Maxine remembers that feeling – of belonging, of knowing anyone can win if they really want it – like it was yesterday. And she'll always remember, too, that teacher, who would later use her own money to buy Maxine a decent pair of running shoes.

Lessons in business leadership from **Maxine Horne**

The work journey

At 13, Maxine lied about her age to get jobs at the local hairdresser and the corner store. The money she made was put away with any babysitting payments she could jag, and she happily handed over her first pay packet in return for the five snow-white pairs of socks. As aimless as she was bright, her teenage years brought all the angst they usually do, especially when Malcolm and Susan had their own children – Jason (who was born when Maxine was 12) and Anthony (who arrived when she was 14). But Malcolm always had a special place for Maxine.

'I walked on water when it came to my father,' she says. That didn't stop the stormy brawls she had with him, though, or the lack of direction that enveloped her adolescence. Long hours were squandered in her bedroom playing punk music or British ska band Madness too loud, ignoring her parents' refrain to turn it down, and playing the odd day of hooky from school without too much regard for whether she'd be caught or not. Maxine was saved by a natural, inquiring mind, graduating from our Year 12 equivalent with marks that would allow her to study at university, or get one of the local jobs advertised. Despite the love she had for her father and her stepmother Susan, she wanted to escape the life she was assigned, but she was unsure in which direction she should travel. Now, looking back, she knows that ambition – to want a life that she hadn't yet experienced – was her ticket to success. 'I could have been a disaster,' she says.

Thirty-five years later, Maxine Horne has shown time and time again, she's not. Vita Group Limited, the company she calls her 'third child' and in which, as CEO, she owns a 26 per cent stake, boasts 1700 team members (or Vita Peeps as Maxine likes to call them) in more than 160 different locations across Australia. In 2016, the company reported revenues of more than $600 million, up 34 per cent on the previous year.

'My goal has never been to be filthy rich – it was to be better than what I was,' she says candidly. 'I feel somewhat disingenuous to say it's not about the money – being in the position that I'm in – because if I didn't have it, it *would* be about the money.' She knows it is easy for people who have money to say that 'it's not about the money'. 'I get that – but it's not my driver because if it were, I would have left this business when we floated on the stock exchange.'

Neville Threader, from Telstra, has worked with Maxine for more than 20 years. 'She still sometimes arrives in Melbourne dressed in jeans and a T-shirt,' he says. 'I say to her you've been coming here for 20 years, you've got a few dollars in the bank, go down and buy yourself a Burberry coat. She could put it in her bag, put it on when she's cold and it would be stylish. The other day she texted me. She'd got a Burberry coat!' Threader's point highlights her lack of focus on personal riches. 'It took her about two years to get that coat – she's never ever wanted the trappings of wealth.' He says it's only now that she's becoming comfortable with the 'rich' tag.

'She's grown into herself in the sense that she is wealthy, she is successful and she's let herself accept that.'

Maxine says it's what her company and its team can achieve that drives her. 'It might sound egotistical, but I love the thought that I had something positive to do with their lives.'

Maxine's story is a tale of ideas and hard work, of lessons learnt sometimes twice or even three times over, of personal and professional failings, of losing and rediscovering how to win again. It's a tale of thinking smart and running hard. This book represents both her professional and her personal story; the abrupt end of her marriage to David McMahon in January 2013 serving as a beacon for the latter. Until then, David was a part of the Vita Group journey. He left the company with a divorce settlement that included property and shares, and Maxine remains magnanimous about his early role. She was made sole CEO on 30 January 2014. The share market, a tough judge, has shown its faith with the company's share price increasing almost nine times since her appointment.

So how does a kid from Caerphilly, who ambled through school and spurned the chance to attend university, become one of Australia's most successful businesswomen? How does someone with a far-fetched dream to escape her past become a true entrepreneur for the future, one who is able to pioneer change in the rapidly-moving telecommunications industry? How did Maxine Joan Horne travel from Struggle Street in Ipswich, UK, to Millionaires' Row in Brisbane, Australia, turning a meagre annual salary to one that allows bulging property portfolios and jet-setting holidays? And how can others follow her path, navigating the tricks to setting up a business and enjoy the same success?

'I never thought she'd have this,' her stepmother Susan, who now works in Brisbane with Maxine, says. 'We were just ordinary plodders. We wanted the best for our kids but we would never, ever have thought …' Maxine's father Malcolm died in 2000 at the age of 59 of the rare brain disorder supranuclear palsy. He would be in disbelief, Susan says. 'But he'd be so, so proud.'

Susan and Malcolm enjoyed a hint of Maxine's early success during a holiday to Australia a few years after Maxine and David moved here. But back then, there was no public float, no national business footprint, no millions in the bank. Just damn hard work, where Maxine and David would rise before dawn and go to bed after everyone else. To this day Susan struggles to grasp the success her daughter – and they see each other in mother–daughter terms – chiselled out Downunder. 'Whatever she's done, she's excelled at,' Susan says. 'It's that dogged determination.'

Certainly that pluck – to take on a challenge others might not, to want to win handsomely, to be prepared to scrap like a boxer – has been central to Maxine's success. It's helped her build a company from nothing, to rebuild it when a lack of care almost forced it under, and to fatten it up after the lean times waged by the global financial crisis. Maxine relishes a challenge, and knows she doesn't always get it right. Her mistakes fill the pages of this book. But a mistake one day shouldn't lead to stage fright the next, and Maxine uses mistakes as part and parcel of learning. If you take the lesson on offer, she says, you usually win the next time round.

Over the past two decades, Maxine believes she's sometimes adopted the wrong strategy, or the right strategy at the wrong time. She's taken too long to articulate the company's values, pulled the wrong chain in striving to save money, and focused too much on the nitty-gritty of the business at the expense of the big picture. But each time she's stumbled, she's pulled herself up with the lesson she needs to learn, and is happy to defer to others. That's prompted strong personal growth, as she's balanced the task of being the company's chief operating officer with raising two young children, negotiated the nation's elite business scene as a woman, and turned up to work, even as her 23-year marriage crumbled. Now, as sole CEO, she's focused on charting the company's course for the future.

A street fighter

'Maxine's great strength is that she's a street fighter,' Vita Group chairman Dick Simpson, a former Telstra group managing director, a former chair of CSL (Hong Kong's biggest mobile carrier), Telstra Clear and REACH, says. 'She's a straight shooter, she doesn't back down from an argument, and she'll fight and claw for every inch because she doesn't like leaving anything on the table.' Simpson ranks Maxine as one of the best CEOs he's witnessed and says the professional and personal trajectory she's travelled is a showcase for others. Someone from a privileged background might not have fought as hard or kicked as much, he says. He gives the example of early board meetings; testy affairs in the wash-up of the company's public listing, where Maxine believed simple questions about the business amounted to an attack on her professional judgement. Indeed, on being offered the position of board chair, Simpson decided he had to have a one-on-one meeting with Maxine. He wanted to know that she was prepared to change, and to learn. He told her that her answer might dictate whether or not he accepted the job. She didn't flinch.

'She immediately said yes,' Simpson says, a testament to her willingness to soak up knowledge and perform at a higher level. 'And she wanted to know where she should start.' He cites an executive study on derailment done years ago, which showed that the inability to grow often hampers talented people. He says the study focused on the 'shining stars' who raced up the career ladder early, but never made it to the top office. 'There were a lot of a reasons, but one predominant reason that came through was that their greatest strength, as they moved up in an organisation, became their greatest weakness.'

Certainly it was Maxine's take-no-prisoners approach that marked her out from the day she started work, post-school, at Barclays, the British multinational banking and financial services company. Maxine had applied for the three-year management internship, where young school leavers were piloted through different departments while still at school. Her marks would have allowed university entry, but she shunned that, along with opportunities to join the West Merseyside Police and the British Army. In part, she rejected those because her teachers suggested she take them. Maxine wanted to make it on her own, and like most teenagers, believed she knew best. So, instead, she started work at Barclays in Bargoed, a town on the Rhymney River, straddling the ancient boundary of Monmouthshire and Glamorgan.

Each day, she'd take the 40-minute bus ride to work, returning each afternoon. She'd save most of her money, as her grandparents taught her, but would occasionally splash out on music: cassettes and vinyl recordings of punk rock, Meat Loaf, Madness, and anything else that took her fancy in the grey days of early 1980s Britain. It was the era that saw the rise of Margaret Thatcher and the conflict created by her dry economic policies that ultimately delivered the nation its current prosperity. Pre-Walkman, pre-CD and pre-digital recordings that allow entire libraries to be carried on the small phones Maxine now sells, music was the antidote and Maxine would play hers loud and long into the night. It erased the boredom of her day job, which involved, in her words, 'stuffing statements into envelopes and making tea for a branch of about 50 people, three times a day'.

'My biggest claim to fame was the time I created a riot because I decided not to make the tea.' This story risks painting Maxine as querulous; an upstart who believed she was too good to be doing menial tasks. Certainly many of her superiors saw it like that. But there was more to it. To this day, she questions everything. Why are we doing that? Why can't we do this? Is there another way? It's a habit she's had her since her first job, and it usually prompts a better outcome, as it did back then.

'I said I'm not making the tea today,' she says. 'It's a waste of time and there should be a roster.' Context is important here. Bargoed, which means border, is tiny and many of Barclays staff did not fit the bill of being management trainee blow-ins; most were locals who had worked their way up to senior positions over the years, and in some cases, decades. Maxine Horne, 17, was challenging what they had done day in, day out, forever. She had stopped their morning cuppa, and her refusal to give in led a hasty path to her manager's office. There, she didn't take a step back either. It was more productive, she told him, for her to do other tasks, and each person to make their own tea or coffee – or for staff to take turns. Perhaps it was easier to give in, or perhaps Maxine's logic won out, but a week later, a small roster was posted in the office kitchen.

Challenging the status quo had worked. Tick. It was a reminder of running around that track, at school, beating the rich girls. Never accept what others might think as inevitable.

Upwards and onwards

After 18 months at Barclays and Barclaycard, and a few other small companies, Maxine joined Mercury Communications Ltd, followed by its subsidiary Mercury Paging, in November 1987. We can all look back as we grow older and find those markers that help colour our personal histories. Meeting a partner, having a child, moving to a new city, or a traumatic event might prompt us to re-evaluate our path. For Maxine, it was the job at Mercury Paging that proved a turning point, personally and professionally, and the first rung on a career ladder that would reach giddy heights more than a decade later in Australia.

At first, Maxine held the post of sales executive dealing with the government sector. Her duties involved selling the benefits of Mercury Communications over British Telecom. At Mercury, her focus was wide-area radio paging, and she was tasked with handling all major accounts. It's where she met her first and predominant career mentor – Tricia Mittens. Back then, she was Tricia Wilson, and she became the company's national sales manager. Tricia soon found that Maxine Horne had been earmarked, by her predecessor, as one of those sales executives that should be 'let go'.

'Her name was on the wrong side of the line – the side that said she was not going to make it,' Tricia says. 'But I wanted to make up my own mind.' Tricia was young and sassy and dressed impeccably, with the trademark 1980s shoulder pads and killer heels. 'Maxine was a sponge and the reason it wasn't working before was because no-one was giving her the direction she needed.' That's true, but it's not the whole picture. Tricia provided a role model for Maxine; a signpost of what she could be, if she just learnt how. Maxine listened to everything Tricia said, followed it to the letter, and worked harder and longer. Within 18 months she was promoted to regional sales manager for the north of England, where six senior account executives reported to her. More than that, though, sales became a passion. She loved the thrill of the chase and the feeling of triumph. It ticked every box. Maxine got noticed, and acknowledged.

'I wonder if Tricia hadn't have been there what I'd be doing now,' Maxine says today. It's a rhetorical question. 'I really wonder that. And that's had a huge influence on how I run this business. I talk about the power of a leader, you have no idea the value that you can add, not just to someone at work, but to their whole life. Tricia really believed in me.'

Self-belief. Tick. Work hard. Tick. Be a sponge and soak up every trick you can. Tick. Tick. Tick.

It was at Mercury Paging that Maxine also met David McMahon, the big-talking, big personality salesman, whom she would go on to marry in June 1990. Life moved at a fast and colourful pace. Her management post at Mercury Paging led to her being headhunted for a senior accounts manager post with Vodapage Ltd and then Hutchinson. 'I'm not very proud of that last one,' she admits. 'I took the job more for the money more than for job satisfaction. It confirmed my view that people rarely choose a job for money alone.'

Both Maxine and David talked, often, about escaping the UK climate and setting up home in David's native New Zealand, but a stopover in Brisbane on the way to the 1990 Commonwealth Games in Auckland sealed their fate and two years later, in May 1992, the Queensland capital became their new base. It was here, in Australia, that the lessons Maxine had already learnt – about challenging the status quo, believing in herself, working harder than everyone else and the triumph of victory – laid the groundwork for big dividends.

Lessons learnt

The business gaffes Maxine has made throughout her career – and there have been many – are chronicled in the following pages. It is Maxine's intention that others learn from her mistakes, no matter what industry they're in. Like any successful business, hers started with an idea, a seed that was fertilised into a service or a product that people wanted and were prepared to buy.

For Maxine, the idea was to connect mobile phones to the Optus network, rather than physically selling handsets, the dominant business approach at the time. That was the idea, or the seed. But few ideas are new, and it was Maxine's experience in the UK that guided much of her early success here in Australia. In the

UK, in the early 1990s, mobile phones were becoming consumer items, readily available in retail shopping centres. In Australia, they remained a niche product, used for business, and sold predominantly in industrial areas. After a trip to the UK, Maxine and David decided to open their first mobile phone retail store – and what she believes to be Australia's first, in the middle of a shopping centre.

Maxine remembers how some people, particularly centre lease managers, scoffed at them, but they pushed forward nevertheless. In many ways, their determination was driven more by an ignorance of the pitfalls ahead than any innate understanding or specialist knowledge of what was actually involved. If they had known, they probably would have ensured that the blue and orange paint was dry before opening that first Pacific Fair store! They might have had a well-considered and articulated strategy to deal with the phenomenal response that followed the opening. They certainly would have had spare stock, and they would have earmarked the next centre where a store should be opened. And the next. But they didn't.

'It was ridiculous,' Maxine says now. 'Phones were just flying out the door. It was an overnight success.'

Indeed, within a year, Maxine and David had opened other stores in Queensland, as well as in Victoria and NSW. But their business model was largely drafted on the run. They paid themselves a simple salary, and as they made a profit in one store, they used it to open the next. Maxine ordered the stock, drawing columns on blank pieces of A3 paper, to ensure their records were kept up to date. All receipts were taken home and put into shoeboxes until tax time. It was a game of business catch-up, and Maxine and David thrived on it.

'Sleep came second to everything else. We just worked and worked and worked,' she says. And all the time, their company's bank balance grew and grew and grew.

Today Maxine will tell you the significance of having a well-planned and executed strategy; of the need to know how, when and where to open a new business; the importance of looking after your team, particularly in hard times; the need to articulate the values of your business well and ensure the culture puts them into practice. All of that sits at the heart of the Vita Group, but she's had to play catch-up since the day the ribbon was cut at that first Pacific Fair store. In part, that was because of the phenomenal growth of Fone Zone (which later became Vita Group), but it was also because she was learning what to do – and what not to do – on the hop.

As customers walked out of that first Gold Coast store with phones, Maxine and David didn't have a proper business structure to guide the next step in growing their enterprise. It all lay within their heads. Full stop. Strategy – if you'd call it that – was concocted over breakfast or on the way to day care, and the company's values, which were clear to them, were imparted in an ad hoc way. But that didn't stop Fone Zone's brand new shiny take-off, and it kept gaining altitude. By the end of 1995, the company boasted a dozen stores in three States.

A clear and documented strategy wasn't the only factor missing, though. Due diligence was not top of the list and the couple were taken in by a deal that would make them millionaires one day, but risk them losing their home the next. It taught them that risks need to be chronicled and considered, and that due diligence, even if it slowed a deal or even cost a packet, was worth every cent. It was a new lesson to add to Maxine's folder. Tick. But sometimes, a bit like learning to play the piano, it's only through practice that the importance of the lesson is revealed. And that was the case with the company's purchase of Next Byte. It provided a stark reminder that the need for due diligence, both financial and operational, never expires.

Global financial crisis

The GFC taught all business owners a lesson, and Maxine wasn't exempt there, either. This was a time when everyone, faced with declining profits and no clear exit out, pulled their belts in – customers and companies alike. Maxine says now that she took the easy option, cutting costs and targeting customer and team member benefits that had been an integral part of the culture she had developed. In retrospect, it was the wrong chain to pull, and it's taken years to fix the lower morale and lower service that resulted. To this day, she wishes she had walked in and asked her team whether they would have preferred to keep the benefits – like water coolers in stores, monthly nights out and the ability to offer queuing customers a free coffee – or take a 10 per cent pay cut. She's pretty sure they would have picked the latter.

The need to look outside at trends in other industries or even other countries has provided buckets of money to the company's bottom line. The inspiration for the extended warranty offer and an express replacement service contributed millions each year and came out of a conversation with a salesperson at a major Australian retailer. Maxine was offered an extended warranty for the vacuum cleaner she had just purchased. She declined, but walked away determined it was something Fone Zone should also offer. The idea behind CARE – the company's all-encompassing customer focus framework – followed an irritating exchange between Maxine and a cosmetics saleswoman at a large department store. The central tenet of Queensland Network Options (QNO) – their first business – came from a chat with a work friend, and their profitable decision to sell mobile phones in shopping centres replicated what was happening back in the UK.

Many of the lessons chronicled in this book are raw, showing both Maxine's candour and her determination to share what she's learnt with others. She is able to pinpoint an emotional outburst as a young mother working until midnight each night as the flag for their decision to finally extend the business beyond their family by appointing a financial controller. That first hiring forced Fone Zone to develop a structure, particularly a finance structure, that encouraged sustainability. But Shiu Chand, who took the job after seeing it advertised in *The Courier-Mail*, had his work cut out for him.

'I remember Maxine coming in and shutting the door and saying, "Shiu, can you explain this dividend policy?",' he says now. This was in 1995 and he admits to being surprised. But that's often how family businesses work: owners need to see their business as an entity, where they filled the role of director and shareholder. 'It's normal in a family-owned company, at that level, to see it only as their company and their money,' he says. Chand introduced internal structures and the discipline of a structured salary package for the couple. But a bigger shock came when he asked Maxine to provide all the accounts. She did so willingly, bringing to work the next day shoeboxes brimming with receipts. 'It was all manually done,' Chand says. 'It was like a computer or information file. I'd ask a question and she'd say it would be filed in there – in a shoebox!' Maxine says Shiu had the ability never to look shocked, despite her also handing over pages and pages of A3 paper, with neatly drawn columns, accounting for every purchase she had made.

Chand's appointment seems a lifetime ago, but the importance of picking the right team members has been crucial to the company's success. It's something Maxine has had to learn too; her loyalty to team members who failed to cut it sometimes stood in the way of moving forward. All team members are made a promise when they join the company: they will leave with more skills than when they arrived.

Ben Johnson joined in 2002 and rose quickly through the ranks. Twelve years later, Maxine tapped him on the shoulder at a company dinner. 'You know what, Ben,' she said. 'It's probably time that you moved on and got some experience somewhere else.'

Ben remembers every word. 'I was gutted, absolutely gutted,' he says. 'I had given her a third of my life and she was ending it.' Having moved on in his career, Ben now knows it was the right decision. There is no ill feeling; just respect. 'In hindsight it really was the right thing to do. It was one of those tough love things.'

Setting an example

Maxine Horne gets involved in her employees' lives in a way most CEOs steer clear of, and she makes no apology for it. She will counsel colleagues during hard times and go out dancing with them on a Friday night. She reprimands them if they celebrate too hard at a post-work function and tries to ensure they live by the business values that are plastered across the walls of Vita Group's Brisbane office.

Luke Wadeson started as a part-time salesman at

Chermside in the city's northern suburbs, and 14 years later, boasts the position of ICT Specialist Enterprise. He nominates three chief influences in his life so far – 'my mum, my dad and Maxine'. It's not something you expect from a 35-year-old employee, but he's not alone. 'The thing that always sticks with me is that Maxine consistently highlights our core values. It's now what I live by: I'm a walking, talking version of our core values.' Others say the same.

That hands-on approach, where Maxine sees the company as her own even after its public listing, has had to be finessed along the way. She remembers, in the wake of almost going bust back in 1996, noticing a stockpile of Post-it notes in the stationery cupboard.

'Who ordered Post-it notes?' she bellowed. 'From now on, no more Post-it notes!' She grabbed a pack of paper from the copy machine, which had text on one side. 'I turned them all over and stapled them and said, "There's your bloody Post-it notes!".' She bursts out laughing now, explaining that the story has taken on mythical proportions. But really she's trying to hide her embarrassment.

The transition from giving birth to her 'third child' to publicly listed company has been gut-wrenching at times. It's hard to let go, in the same way parents of teenagers will lure them home with offers of doing their washing and a home-cooked meal. It's a journey that continues, and in the pages that follow, Maxine charts both the triumphs and the pitfalls.

Natural business flair

Lessons don't always have to be learnt the hard way, and Maxine's natural business acumen has afforded her, and her company, other quick paths to success. Following the customer 'ant trail' is one of those and each time Maxine and her leadership team look for a new venture, they study its geography. Is it in a good shopping area? (It needs to be.) How accessible is the parking? (It needs to be good too.) Is the available retail space close to the centre's entrance? (That's not so good because people will walk straight by, determined to deal with the issue that prompted their visit.) The list of 'dos' and 'don'ts' goes on, but Maxine has spent hours and hours sitting in shopping centres watching customers, like ants, go about their daily tasks. It's not a new concept. Real estate agents often advise buying the worst house in the best street, but the adherence to that rule has helped Fone Zone, and later Vita Group, enormously. On the few occasions when it didn't follow that trusty ant trail, the profits stopped.

That same method has helped Vita Group roll out close to 100 Telstra stores in less than four years. The right to do that is at the centre of a licence agreement between the two companies which grants Vita Group the power to brand its stores as Telstra outlets. The agreement was drafted as Vita Group opened stores across the nation in a short period. That project involved hundreds of team members focused on minute detail. Some 120 different tasks – from negotiating leases to hiring sales teams to organising rosters – are involved when a new store opens.

'We are Telstra,' Pete Connors, Vita Group's chief operating officer, says as a way of explaining the company's current footprint. 'We're a big franchise.' The roll-out – itself a lesson in effective project management – was executed with military precision. Connors says the 120 different tasks are assigned and plotted, and someone is made responsible for each one of them. 'They should all then occur in a certain flow – in a typical project-management way.' In another lesson, Connors says it was Vita Group's 'small store mentality' and the attention to detail it brings that allowed for a successful roll-out.

No doubt exists that Maxine Horne has grown alongside the company she now leads: from the kid who wanted to belong, to the salesperson who wanted to win, to the mother who wanted to both pack the school lunches and run the show. Along the way, she's learnt the worth of good friends and daily exercise, and of living the values that money can't buy; those very values her grandparents Rose and George taught her as a six year old.

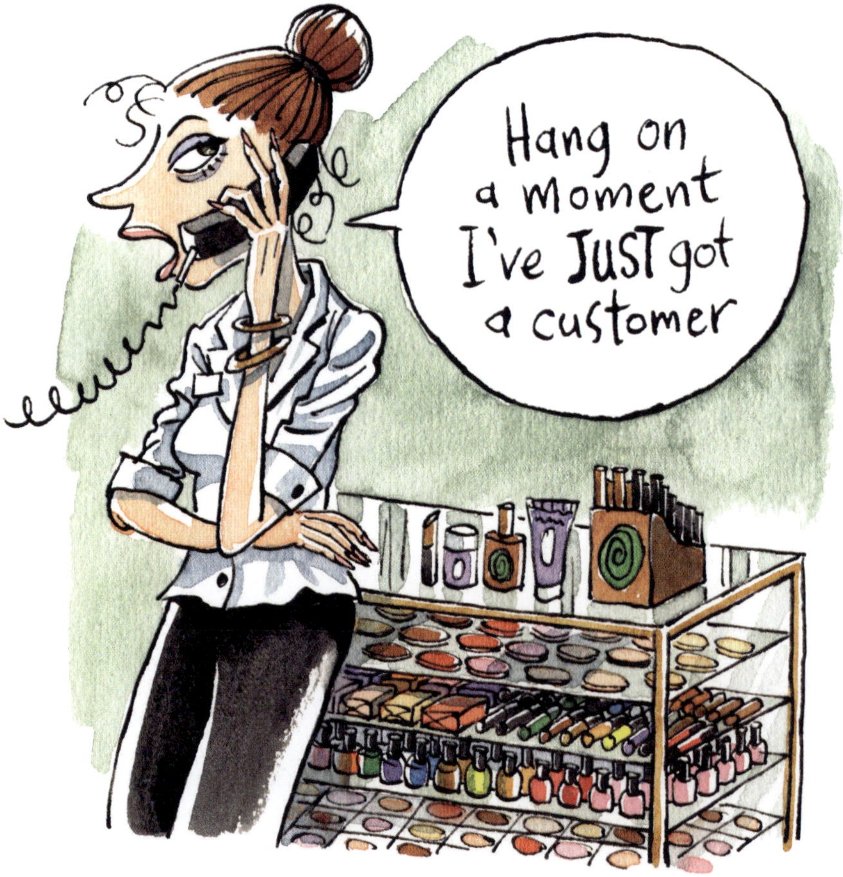
Hang on a moment I've JUST got a customer

1.
Customer is King (or Queen)

'If you work just for money, you'll never make it, but if you love what you're doing and you always put the customer first, success will be yours.' – McDonald's founder Ray Kroc

It's a Saturday morning in 1996, and Maxine Horne has gone from launching an idea to running a business, riding the wave of Australia's love of the mobile phone. The company owned by Maxine and her husband David McMahon – Fone Zone Pty Ltd – was less than a year old, but they already boasted stores in three Australian States. Life was busy, and exciting. Dragging David and her toddler son Jack through Brisbane's Indooroopilly shopping centre, Maxine headed towards the cosmetics counter of a major department store. She was targeting a particular mascara made by Lancôme, and she knew where to get it, and exactly how much it should cost. She bounded up to the counter, ready to do a deal. The shop assistant stood chatting on a store phone. It sounded like a personal call.

'I stood there trying to get her attention and then in the end I heard her say, "Hang on a moment. I've just got a customer". But she didn't disconnect!'

Almost two decades later, Maxine's indignation with that assistant remains.

'I asked whether I could get this particular mascara and she said, "Oh, it's out the back", as though that was a hamper to me buying it. "I'll have to go and get it."' Maxine heard the emphasis she put on every word – and it sounded like 'you-are-putting-me-out-ma'am'.

'Yes, that would be good,' Maxine replied, before waiting patiently for the return of the attendant and the mascara she wanted. 'By then I was getting pretty shitty. Anyway, she came back with it and I purposely let her ring it up – which was quite mean of me, really – and then she went to take my money and I said, "Look, I've changed my mind. I'm not going to buy it but I want you to know the reason why. It's not the price. I'm happy to pay that. It's not the product. I want this mascara.

It's not the packaging. Nor is it your fit-out. It's not your lighting either." By this time the shop assistant was listening, wondering what was coming next. The phone sat, waiting to be tended, her friend presumably ready to pick up where they had left off. "The sole reason I'm not buying this mascara today is because of you and the way you treated me."

'Then I grabbed Jack and I'll always remember David saying to me, "Does this mean we have to keep on shopping?"'

Maxine walked away wondering whether any of her team would treat a customer in the same way. The episode only took 15 minutes, but it played on her mind and fitted with something she had heard at a conference where the guest speaker had his audience in the palm of his hand. Maxine was sitting in one of the front rows.

'He was saying that by adding value you earn the right to charge more. He talked about a home security business where employees would lay a cloth down and use a portable vacuum cleaner because they'd done their research and discovered that people found it irritating that workmen would come, do the work, and then leave a mess. That got me thinking – what are the things that irritate our customers?'

Maxine knew how quickly her trip to buy mascara had turned sour, and with the company's 1996 conference looming, she decided to target customer service. The agenda was scrapped and the two-day ideas fest focused instead on the best way to wow customers.

'We were looking for an idea and I wasn't going to be in the store every day delivering it, so I wanted everyone to come up with the best idea and own it,' Maxine says. Over the next two days, they explored customer service – coming up with ideas that no-one else offered but that could also serve as the rationale for charging more. On the first day, there were no limits, and someone joked about giving each new customer the keys to a Ferrari. On day two, reality was enforced. What was possible? What might work? What would have synergies with their business? What were those important things – big or small – that others in the industry were not offering? Team members worked in groups, with three limitations imposed. Those related to cost, time and practicality.

'So the Ferrari idea went,' Maxine says, 'but we got a dozen things that would really work.'

The result? A list of how customer would be treated when they walked into a Fone Zone store. It was called the CARE program, and stood for 'Customers Are Really Everything'. The list of ideas ran over several pages; small gestures with the aim of making each customer feel special. Customers would be greeted within 30 seconds. They would be offered a chair if they had to wait an extended period of time. Simple toys and colouring books would be provided so children could play while their parents discussed phones. Now it seems common sense, but it wasn't back then, and CARE – which remains 21 years later in more sophisticated forms – is the bedrock of how the company plans, coaches, develops its people and engages with its communities.

Back in the mid-1990s, anyone who bought a mobile phone had to take it home and charge it overnight, let it run down and then recharge it. Remember? It was a laborious process – but it was the only way you could make your first call. Fone Zone's CARE program included a solution for that too. Customers would be given two options: they could buy phones which were pristine and untouched in their box; or they could buy phones which Fone Zone team members had unpacked, charged, and had ready to go. In nine cases out of 10, customers bought the pre-charged phone. They could also opt to have their message bank set up and any emergency contacts pre-loaded.

The CARE program tried to ensure each phone was tailored to each customer. In sales jargon, it's called 'consultative selling', and it would begin with the customer being asked several questions about how they might use the phone. Who else in your family has one? Do you use it during the day or in the evening?

'The questions were aimed at us trying to identify the kind of phone or the type of features they would like,' Maxine says. 'It would also indicate what type of plan they should have. Remember this is 1996, and if you used the phone predominantly at night you got cheaper rates. You could also connect to someone and get free text messaging, and so on. We soon learnt that our industry is confusing, and we saw it as our role to remove the confusion. We had a tagline – it's a very succinct tagline – I'm joking: "More Mobile for your Money with Less Confusion, Guaranteed". And if we didn't do that, we'd pay the customer $5.'

Another consumer care idea adopted was taken from high-end fashion stores like Louis Vuitton or Carla Zampatti; something quite small but which shoppers also notice. At those stores, the purchase is packed nicely and then the attendant walks around the counter and presents the customer with the bag. It is never passed across the counter.

'It's the intangible things that work,' Maxine says. 'So we had this thing – you always put it in a bag and you always walked it round the counter and told the customer what you'd done. You would give them a card and ensure that if they had any problems they knew they were welcome to come back.'

Over the years, the CARE program has been moulded and updated. Seamless upselling was included, mirroring what happens when you visit a car dealership. Once a car is purchased, you're offered coffee, and while sitting there enjoying your coffee and your new purchase, a finance specialist might join in. Someone might then suggest your car windows could be tinted, or new wheels fitted. Maxine took the same approach in running the Vita Group. The business manager's job is not to do the sale, but to take a step back and observe the sale, and ensure that the customer's purchase was truly personalised to them.

Metrics play a huge role now, but back in 1996, the

whole interaction between sales teams and customers was evaluated by 'mystery shoppers', who would be employed by an outside company to purchase a mobile phone.

'But they were never mystery-shopped on the sale itself,' Maxine stresses. 'They were mystery-shopped on the customer service. And that allowed us to know how our customer service program was working.'

One of the changes to the CARE program was an attempt to standardise the service that was being offered. 'My idea of customer service is very different to yours – it's very subjective,' Maxine says. 'But if it was the very basis for our culture, we had to ensure it worked across the business in some consistent way.' That also allowed the leadership team to explain the elements of the CARE program and how it should be used. 'For example, let's take the one about greeting the customer within 30 seconds with a smile. That meant that if you turned up to work with a crappy attitude you should be prepared for your leader to have a discussion with you before you even hit the retail floor. You hear everybody say the customer is always right, but it's true, and the easiest way to overcome a conflict with a customer is to agree with them. It is very hard to argue with someone when they are not arguing with you. It also displays empathy.'

Maxine says the CARE program worked because it was scripted by those employed to deliver it. 'The most important thing was that I didn't come up with that. The team did,' she says. On the back of her mascara story.

Rebecca McLeod, Vita Group's general manager (projects), says customer care is 'part of the DNA of the organisation' and was the basis for Fone Zone being able to distinguish itself within the industry. 'You just knew when you went into a Fone Zone store that you were going to get good service,' she says. While the success was originally tracked through mystery shopping, other metrics (such as prospect conversion rate, average transaction value and customer advocacy scores) were later used. Tweaks have been made over the years, including a rigorous training program for every single employee, Australia wide, across all company brands. That was a recognition that constant coaching is at the heart of all improvement – no matter what the topic. 'It became a sort of refocus on what CARE means both internally (to our team members) and externally (to our customers),' McLeod says.

Every team member receives instructor-led training, one-on-one coaching and online modules, and as members progress through the organisation, a tailored education program is added. For example, a store manager (or business manager as Vita Group refers to them because they are taught to run a business and not just sell) will have also undertaken a workshop built around every aspect of the business, and then further time in another store shadowing another business manager. Coaching, at all levels, is an integral part of training, and is tracked store by store, area by area, State by State, on a daily basis.

The first step happens before the doors open when team members prepare for each customer interaction. It takes about 15 minutes, around a whiteboard, or with their personal tablets, talking about the specific focus for that day's trading. This is an area for the whole team to focus on. For example, next Monday the focus might be 'Asking Open Questions'. The retail business manager will then lead his or her team on a speedy role play about great open questions to drive a good customer conversation. Everyone is involved. Once that preparation is completed, and any questions answered, the front door is opened for business – and a step-by-step program commences with each customer. For retail customers the steps are: Approach, Question, Match, Close, Own.

1. Approach

How do you approach the customer? This is considered a key component because it sets the tone for the rest of the conversation and puts the customer at ease. It never starts with a 'Hello Madam, what can I do for you today?'. Rather the approach, customer service teams are taught, should begin with a smile and a personal or individual question. Perhaps something like, 'Great jacket, where did you get that from?' Or 'I see you're flat out with the kids today!' Or 'Hope you found it easy to park in this rain?'

'The rules are that it be individually tailored to the customer and that it be non-business,' McLeod says. 'This is the task, mainly, of the store greeter, the person who meets each customer at the store's entrance. Their job is then to find the customer's first point of call; who they need to see. This time the questions will be more direct, and business-related. For example, "What brings you in to our store today?" Once the greeter knows the answer, they direct that customer to stage two of the process, where a team member is ready to help.'

2. Question

This stage is key to the entire conversation, as it is where the team member learns about the customer and their needs. If this part of the process is under-done or done poorly, the customer leaves the store without their needs being fully met. The salesperson will ask a broad range of questions that must be focused on the individual and how they can be helped – not on pushing a product. With that knowledge, they move to stage three.

3. Match

This stage requires the sales team member to match products and value-added services to the needs uncovered during the questioning stage. For example, 'I think this tablet is most suitable for your needs.' Or 'I would recommend this plan.' But that's just the first step. Conversation has been flowing, and this presents additional opportunities. 'I see the crack in your current phone … maybe you need a tougher phone case?' Or 'Have you seen the new selfie stick? I love them.'

4. Close

Once the match is completed, the salesperson moves to 'close', ensuring that they have covered everything that brought the customer to the store that day. This closes the transaction process, ensuring the customer has had all their needs met.

5. Own

The final step requires the salesperson to 'own' the customer, and that's what happens once the customer leaves the store. The transaction becomes personal. It might mean calling the customer the next day and asking how they've found their new phone, or recommending – or even downloading – a few apps that could help them at home or in their business.

•

Every retail business has its own version of customer service programs, each with their own acronym. Starbucks, the coffee chain, developed its LATTE program after it discovered one of its greatest risks was dealing with inevitable conflicts when orders were mixed up. LATTE taught Starbucks employees to Listen, Acknowledge, Take Action, Thank The Customer and Explain The Problem. According to author Charles Duhigg, it uses this model to role-play potential issues so that an employee in conflict with a customer is on familiar turf. Westfield, the Australian shopping centre giant, has its 10 commandments, a guide to its centre managers to make customers 'welcome in our town'.

Rebecca McLeod says there is nothing fancy in Vita Group's model. 'It's just about consistent application and a few little tweaks – like the non-business greeting.' And she says it is constantly being improved to better fit the company and its customers. One of those improvements involved giving team members online sales journals. Each employee has a tablet, and a series of metrics or measurements – from the number of sales to when their next coaching session is due – can be captured live. They use their journals as both a personal coaching tool and a career development tool. Training workshops are held for team members, and tools like mind maps are taught. However, an employee's mindset is the most critical tool.

'That's the most important thing that you walk in the door with and that's why we hire for will not skill,' McLeod says. 'If you have the right mindset, we can teach you everything else. We often talk about "above the line" versus "below the line" thinking. Above the line is taking responsibility for your actions – and we encourage that constantly. Below the line is where you blame others for your actions. If the mindset is right, the behaviour and results will follow.'

The customer focus is magnified by Vita Group's growing retail range. It has diversified and that's brought a complexity which makes the sale more technical. The five-part process above aims to simplify that.

'The art of being simple in a technical environment is very hard,' Maxine says. 'So we use our CARE program to do that.' The phone is just the vehicle now. 'Ultimately, all a customer might care about is that the calendar works and links to her email or that she can Skype her children. That's what we need to be talking about. That's where we need to be.'

CARE is now so embedded that it has become the bedrock of the company's operating rhythm. Today, the leadership team sees CARE as setting Vita Group apart from its competitors. 'It's the way we plan and coach, offer personalised service and engage with our community,' Pete Connors says.

In Maxine's Words

'Customers want service. Irrespective of age, they go shopping looking for both value and service. The modern day customer is more educated too, particularly in the telco and technology areas, and that means they will do a whole lot of research before they even make a purchase. It also means that they know when someone is not being honest with them – and, trust me, they can spot someone giving them a bit of bullshit a mile away.'

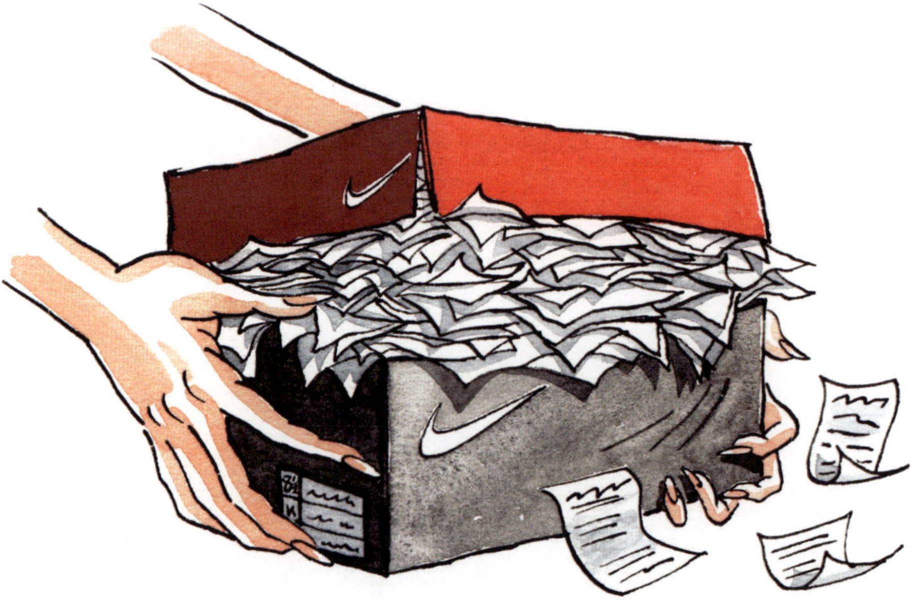

2.

You Don't Know It All

'An expert is someone who has succeeded in making decisions and judgements simpler through knowing what to pay attention to and what to ignore.' – Edward de Bono

Maxine and David were standing in a backyard, sharing a beer and a barbecue with friends. Fone Zone had taken off in 1995 and 1996, and they were now, a year or two later, enjoying the company of industry friends. They didn't socialise often, frequently working from 5 am until midnight, and this was work of sorts too, as the conversation turned to new opportunities. Discussion centred on margins, and then profits, and to dividend policies, as the small business owners told their own stories. One quipped their dividend policy had just peaked at 150 per cent, meaning they were taking one and a half times annual profit out of the business, knowing the cash would keep flowing.

'What's yours, Maxine?' someone asked.

She looked at her friends blankly. She didn't have a clue what they were talking about. 'Then they explained what a dividend was and how at the end of the year you basically take some of the profit out of the business. I asked them whether that was how they made money out of their own business because at that point I didn't really understand how some people seemed to be dripping with money and we weren't, and we were working all night and all day.'

The story highlights both Maxine's brutal honesty and a lack of understanding that often envelops the owners of start-ups as they navigate their way from an idea into a fully-fledged, successful operation.

The next day, Maxine walked into the office of her newly minted financial controller Shiu Chand. 'We need to speak about our dividend policy,' she said.

His response was quick. 'I wondered when you were going to find out about that.'

In hindsight, Maxine's naivety helped grow Fone Zone. Because she was not aware you could pull the money out, it was left to feed the business.

Shiu Chand was Maxine and David's first expert

hiring, a decision that came earlier that year when the business, which was quickly acquiring stores, was taking up every waking hour. At the time, they were living on a property at Burbank, on Brisbane's outskirts; their eldest child Jack was only a baby. One night, as they drove home, the heavens opened and it started pouring with rain. It reminded Maxine of 'Haystack in the Floods', an old French poem chronicling the French Revolution which her high school English teacher had performed in class over and over again. In the poem, the protagonist is mourning, and the weather is mourning with her.

> *She rode astride as troopers do;*
> *With kirtle kilted to her knee,*
> *To which the mud splash'd wretchedly;*
> *And the wet dripp'd from every tree*
> *Upon her head and heavy hair,*
> *And on her eyelids broad and fair;*
> *The tears and rain ran down her face.*

'It sounds so silly now but I was struggling to keep my eyelids open and it's raining and I'm looking out the window thinking how often does it rain in Brisbane? Even the weather is coming out in sympathy with me.' Any new mother who continues to work full time will understand the torment of too much work and too little sleep. Maxine turned to David. 'I can't do this anymore – we have to give this up.'

Context is crucial here. Maxine and David were the

business and Fone Zone, their business, was them. It was a child, in many ways, and demanded attention both night and day. Their company. Their decisions. Their risk. They ran plans and decisions by each other, not other people. Absolutely no structure existed at this stage: no senior management, no chief financial officer, no company lawyer. There was no chief operating officer or marketing arm. 'We simply did everything,' Maxine says. 'We had people at store level, but all the back of office was essentially me.' David urged her to think about her declaration overnight, knowing they had worked too hard to throw it all in. They took a week off – which they had never done previously – and began a conversation about whether they should continue, and if they did, what help they could muster.

'I am a pro and con person,' Maxine says. 'I did my list with all the pros down one side and the cons down the other and we discussed it. We were looking at how do we get out of this business. But we came to the conclusion that there was real opportunity here and we would be stupid to walk away.' That meant, however, they had to radically change what they were doing. 'We realised we had to surround ourselves with people who are better than what we are and who can do the jobs that we can't.'

One of those was the role of financial controller, and so an advertisement was placed in *The Courier-Mail*.

Shiu Chand, who had migrated from Fiji in 1994, a year earlier, applied, and was quickly installed at a desk in head office, or the support centre as it is called. Of course, Maxine and David had other employees, but their focus had been on sales, which was also the skill base of the business owners. This was different. They needed to share the company, in a sense; they needed to have others who they would seek advice from as they sought to grow. Chand joined Fone Zone in 1995 and remained for six years, until Investec Wentworth's private equity team was brought in to advise Maxine and David, taking the business on a journey to raising additional capital.

Up to this point, Maxine was responsible for the back office. She did the accounts and was both fastidious and old-fashioned in how they were done. 'I'll bring the accounts in tomorrow,' she told Chand soon after he started. And that itself was telling. The accounts were kept at home, so she could add to them after her day in the office was over. That night, she got them all together and the next morning she handed them over.

'I don't understand,' Chand said. 'These are the accounts?'

'Yes,' Maxine replied. 'Tomorrow I'll bring the invoices in.'

Chand sat staring at the piles and piles of A3 paper that now filled his desk. In Maxine's handwriting, the lines were filled with neat columns. He picked up one relating to furniture. There, listed, was all the furniture in the office. Chairs. Tables. Desks. Bookcase. Coffee table. The list went on. In the next column was the purchase price. It looked as though it had been completed daily, so there were dozens of additions photocopied neatly and stapled on to the next. 'I was so proud the columns added up,' Maxine said. 'He never showed his dissatisfaction though. He just looked at me and repeated, "I don't understand."'

The next day, Maxine arrived with the invoices. Boxes and boxes of them. Shoeboxes to be precise, packed full of paperwork. Nothing lost. Everything kept. Maxine piled them up on Chand's desk, proud as punch.

'At this point Shiu probably wondered whether he should have answered the advertisement at all,' Maxine says.

He took his time, looking at one shoebox and then the next. 'I don't really understand how you are operating this business,' he said.

'What do you mean?' Wasn't it clear to him? Maxine hadn't lost a thing. Chand asked her to sit down and explain the thought process and the planning behind the decision to open a new store. 'I said we take the bank statement and if there's enough money we do it, and if there's not, we wait a bit,' she says now, laughing. 'He confiscated the cheque book off us that day.'

Shiu Chand, in his deliberate, respectful way, was surprised that Maxine had been able to build the company without basic understandings of how the financial structure should work. The dividend story, where Maxine arrived at Chand's door, came in, sat down and simply asked for it to be explained, highlights that. But so does the story of how Maxine handled the financial accounts.

'It's normal in a family-owned company to see it only as their company and their money,' Chand says. But he admits surprise that where some businesses opted for filing cabinets, and others a computer program, Maxine chose shoeboxes. Perhaps it was telling of her frugal upbringing, where she'd use what was available for free rather than spending money on a filing cabinet.

These days, Maxine is surrounded by a leadership team that makes those significant decisions. In several cases they came with a plan to remain for six months or a year and are still there. Pete Connors, the chief operating officer, is one. So is the chief financial officer Andrew Leyden. Both say they remain because of the value fit. But back in 1995, the appointment of a chief financial officer or what they termed a financial controller was a big step in a small family business. It was probably even a bigger step in terms of Maxine's psychology. She liked control, more so than David. She wanted to know every decision and how it was made; indeed she wanted to make most of them. Her decision making became pedantic in many ways. It was their business and everything from Post-it notes to pen usage was filed away in her mind.

The Post-it note story, as it's become known, now carries mythological proportions: to some it inspires fear, others a good hearty laugh.

Almost every business has similar tales to tell. Kerry

Packer's demand to a TV control room that a show he found offensive be taken off air immediately gave the programmers at Channel Nine the guidance that set its standards for success. Dick Dusseldorp's personal dedication to safety set standards on his building sites for decades. On the other side, John Elliott's insistence to reduce the quantity of strawberries in IXL jam increased profits but helped damage the brand. Maxine's 'ban' on Post-it notes had no material effect on Fone Zone but its conveyance helped develop a parsimony appropriate for a family company trading on tight margins in a runaway market.

•

It was almost two years later, in 1998, that the company finally stopped operating by paper; a slow process but one which now allows the leadership team to closely analyse and monitor sales. The transformation started with the appointment of a financial controller and continued over the following months with IT and people support. It continued to grow each year, and Wayne Smith's appointment in 2006 added to the expert depth of the company, by helping Maxine and David in terms of a strategy framework and the organisation's capabilities.

The decision to open the family business and its secrets to others made Maxine's life much easier on one hand and much harder on the other. It meant she had to learn to let go and let others make decisions and it was something she struggled with daily. Up until 1998, all 40 store managers reported directly to her. Maxine knew how many mobile phones were sold each day in each store, and would question managers about a slow period. The structure was simple and flat, but Shiu Chand's appointment led to discussions on how a more conventional sales structure could be achieved. Eventually it led to the appointment of area managers, and over time it has grown to the structure that exists today, which has sales team members reporting to a store manager, who reports to an area manager, who reports to a regional manager, who reports to a general manager, all the way up to Pete Connors, Maxine's chief operating officer.

It's easy to dismiss some of this as knowledge someone starting a small business should know. But at what point do you know it is going to be bigger than you envisaged? When do you form the view that it will need to turn from a small family business to a bigger entity, requiring outside capital? How do you determine what knowledge you share and with whom you share it? And how hard is it to let go and let the experts you employ do their job? Those are all questions Maxine and David had to answer.

'I remember we were really freaked out by all this money that we were investing in IT,' Maxine says. Now, those investments have led to the complex and real-time reporting systems that allow the leadership team to monitor its national footprint at any time. But it took a leap of faith too, and a plan. What skills do you offer your own business and what skills do you need to import to make it work? It was this decision – to select a team that allowed broader decision making – that laid the foundations for Vita Group's success today.

Perhaps the hardest part for many business owners is that ability to trust those they employ, without watching over their shoulder every step of the way. With Maxine, it's been slow progression, with setbacks each time someone is employed who doesn't fit the business, and leaps and bounds when the role is filled by someone who not only is better at that area than those who own the business, but fits the ethos and culture too.

'The better skilled people you recruit and the more they demonstrate to you that they can actually do the job, if not better than you, the more you are able to let go,' Maxine says. 'But it's really important that the value set has to be compatible. They have to believe in what you are trying to do with the business and they have to be a cultural fit. If they are not you will not trust them and that means you are all over them and you continue doing their job.'

A decision to change strategy – and follow a path of acquisition – forced Maxine to learn this lesson faster. Greg Robertson was director at private equity bank Investec Wealth when Maxine and David visited Sydney in 2002.

'This fellow called and asked would I meet with them because someone had cancelled on them,' Robertson says now. 'He told me they were a husband and wife team who owned 50 mobile phone stores and they only dealt with Telstra.' Robertson, who later became a non-executive director of the company, thought the meeting would amount to an hour donation of his time, and agreed. 'But when I met with them you couldn't help but be impressed with their passion and focus and strategy. They were a very backable pair.'

That meeting was in December 2002 and it wasn't long before Investec put forward a proposal. Maxine and David knew this was expertise they didn't have, but they were single-minded about what direction the company should travel. The industry was growing too quickly, and new brands were popping up across the country. Greenfield expansion would no longer work and they had to change direction and start acquiring some of those brands. But to do that, they needed to raise money.

'The thing that attracted them to us was that we listened to what they wanted to achieve,' Robertson says.

In 2002, Investec Wealth bought a one-third stake in Fone Zone for $8 million, leaving Maxine and David with the remaining two-thirds. They surrendered part of their business, but had the cash to make it bigger. This ingrained in them that their decisions needed to be shared, and experts in finance and law and human resources were as crucial to growth as the ideas discussed around the breakfast table. Given it was only six years earlier that every decision was made by Maxine and

David, Greg Robertson says the move to create a sound business infrastructure happened fast.

'They put together a company that was really well positioned for growth – strong culture, strong systems, IT systems, and investments in training,' he says. That made his move very profitable – over the next few years, the company trebled its profits without any real additional investment.

The CEO's job is a balancing act: you must trust your team, but you can't be 'all care and no responsibility' and you have to know when to roll up your sleeves and join the troops. You also need absolute clarity around what you expect, and you must know that your leadership team will activate and monitor those expectations constantly. Robertson gives an example of a group of stores in Tasmania that were yet to turn a profit. He and David managed the negotiations, while operationally, Maxine was in charge.

'Maxine can be warm and cuddly, but she has a clear view of her way or the highway,' Robertson says. 'She said to them this is the Fone Zone way of doing things. If you do it, I'll love you. If you don't, piss off.' All six stores turned their revenues around quickly.

Vita Group chair Dick Simpson raises another quandary for the CEO: you have to know when to be loyal, and when the person you employed needs to be let go.

'Maxine certainly has the right balance now,' Simpson says, 'but it has taken us a while.' The reason for that is a trap ready to catch any CEO. Sometimes, in order to be loyal, the CEO wants to promote from inside. But when they discover the appointment isn't working, they find it hard to back down. The other pitfall is bringing in people and then keeping them for too long, despite them being unsuitable for the role. 'Maxine can be very tough, very confrontational, very in-your-face and like a mother hen protecting these people who are not performing well – she is much better balanced with that now. If people aren't performing then she'll tell them. That doesn't mean they have to go, it means they need to improve their performance.'

Frequently, in big companies, CEOs are too scared to have that conversation. This results in senior managers continuing to turn up but getting shut out of key decision making. Invariably, they get annoyed. It's never black and white and this is one of those grey areas where good CEOs stand out.

'You have to manage the grey,' Simpson says. 'Maxine is a fabulous example – probably preferring the world was black and white – but now knowing the reality is that there is a big thing in the middle called grey and that is where most of life is.'

Kendra Hammond, who started working at Fone Zone in 2007, says Maxine was 'omnipresent' at first. 'No matter what you did or where you went, her presence was felt whether she was in the room or not. Initially, that was the only way you could get things done – you had to say this was important to Maxine and you needed to deliver it.' She saw it change over time. She's not alone.

'When I first joined, Maxine would pick some things to micro manage and I'd think why would you want to get involved in that?' Andrew Leyden says. Maxine knows that and sensed the frustration. But she felt that she was handing over her child for others to raise and that didn't sit right. Now, it's easier. The business, like her children, has grown up. 'She doesn't do that any more,' Leyden adds.

In Maxine's Words

'Experts bring a perspective or a knowledge you don't have, and it's common sense that, after a point, the business can only grow with their help. It took me a while to learn that and I wish it hadn't. Once they are part of your team, you need to use them and not jump in, at the first opportunity, and take over if they stumble. That doesn't help you and it doesn't help them. If you've got an expert, take their advice. A couple of years ago, we needed a stronger and more senior focus on marketing, so we brought in Chris Preston, our chief marketing officer. Chris has his work cut out for him every day – because I'm a frustrated marketer. Everyone will make mistakes along the way – that's what makes it interesting – but they are called experts for a reason!'

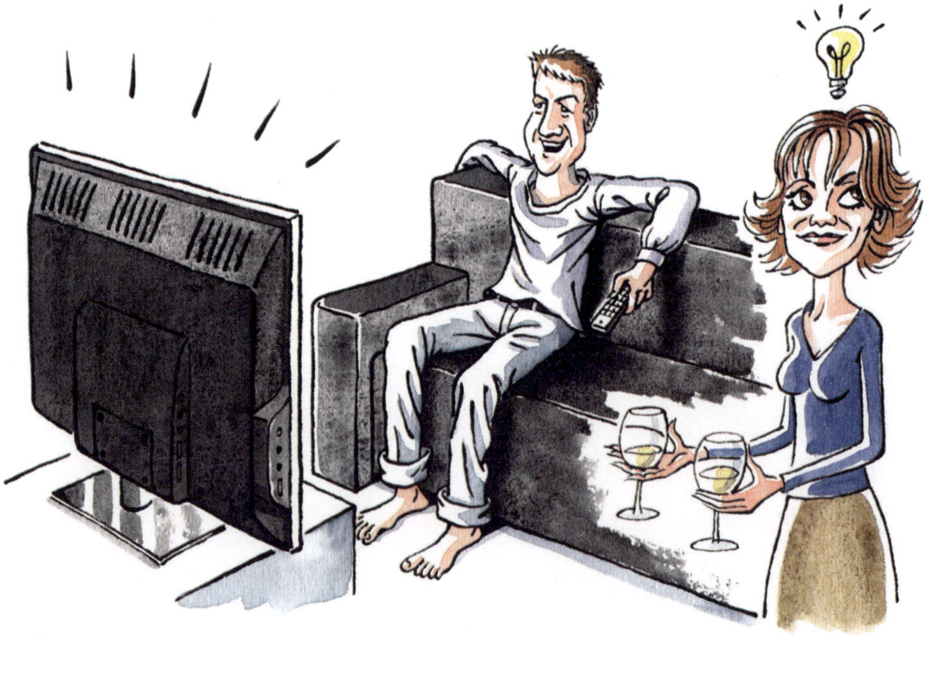

3.

Strategy Rules, OK

'In preparing for battle I have always found that plans are useless but planning is indispensable.' – Former US President and Supreme Commander Dwight D. Eisenhower

Think about the last big function you attended. Perhaps it was a 21st birthday or the celebration of a friend's 40th. Maybe it was a corporate awards night or a company Christmas party. If the event ran seamlessly, with the food, drink and entertainment providing a night to remember, you don't think twice of the strategy or the execution. But if the event doesn't go well, you will most surely remember it. The mistakes will be subject to review. For the errors to be so public, the navel-gazing later may be painful. It's not that much different to what happens in business. Strategy is in the background but it's the foundation on which a business moves forward. A blue-chip company requires a top-notch strategy in order to drive growth – both internally and externally.

For years, Maxine and David carried the strategy for Fone Zone around in their heads. Planning was sometimes done over breakfast or lunch or dinner, on the weekend and weekday nights. Neither really felt the need to jot everything down; they knew it and could articulate it, if needed.

'We would go home and talk about the future of the business,' Maxine says. 'We would talk about the industry, and we would talk about what was going on in the UK because that's where we came from. We'd think this is going to happen and we need to move the business here, and we would come into work and say, "Okay, do this, this, this, this and this". It was not an inclusive strategic model.' Maxine's honesty goes further. 'If I'm perfectly honest, the reason that David and I kept it between ourselves was because we didn't think anyone else could add value ... Now I look back and think that was ignorant and a little bit egotistical too.'

Wayne Smith joined Fone Zone in 2006 after working for Suncorp, Fosters and Coles-Myer. An expert in strategy and organisational capability, he remembers a three-day meeting with Maxine and David soon after he started, where they set a strategy template for the business. Up to that point, it had been done through Maxine's 'presence and style and charisma and personality'. Smith said that worked for a while, but as the company grew, it required proper systems, processes and procedures. One key strategic decision involved working out where in the market Fone Zone wanted to be. Was it in Queensland? Nationally? Internationally? Did it see itself as a retailer? A wholesaler? A distributor?

In 2006, the growth of the company was significant. Stage one, which stretched from the beginnings of the business until financial controller Shiu Chand was appointed, resulted in a dozen store openings in three different States; the first retail chain for mobile phones, and a profitable business. Stage two, which ran until the private equity injection, saw the business grow in terms of customer care; recruitment of experts across finance marketing and IT; the recognition of the importance of culture, and the development of a vision for the company. Stage three ran up until the IPO in 2005, while stage four carried the company forward to the point where the three of them sat in a room, determining its future. In 2009, three years later, Vita Group would negotiate an agreement with Telstra, allowing it to transform its Fone Zone network into 100 Telstra national retail outlets.

Along the way, mistakes were made and strategies faltered; one example being the company's purchase in September 2007 of Next Byte, then Australia's largest authorised Apple reseller. At the time, in the lead-up to September 2007, the factors that led to the global financial crisis were already biting. Some businesses read the economic signs and were tightening their belts. Others were treading water, until they went to the wall. Others, still, wanted to trade their way around it. Fone Zone, which had grown organically for the first stage of its life, was embarking on a strategy of diversification through acquisition. This was a deliberate decision, with the leadership team believing greenfield growth had to be halted and other businesses acquired to broaden its bases. Next Byte appealed. It would add to the company's diversification and it looked like a strong fit.

Apple's reputation and brand were becoming increasingly popular worldwide thanks to the brilliance of its portable music player, the iPod, which excited consumers and allowed them to carry all their music, photos and listen to pre-recorded broadcasts (podcasts) on one device. Computers were getting faster, more powerful, cheaper and more compact and the take-up in the general public was increasing. And Apple had just taken an extra step, the game-changing release of the first iPhone in June 2007 which combined everything the iPod did with an internet-connected phone. The sky seemed all blue.

It now seems a lifetime ago that the Apple shopping experience was not widely available in Australia. But up until 2007 you could only buy an iPod at a big retailer, or Apple computing products through Apple resellers such as Next Byte.

'We were aware of what was happening in America, and its rise there, but we didn't anticipate that the Australian market would soon be flooded with Apple stores,' Maxine says.

Without that knowledge, the purchase of Next Byte – at least in theory – provided a strong market advantage for Fone Zone; it would become the largest dedicated Apple channel in Australia. That ticked a box for David and Maxine and their leadership team. Strategically, it sat well too with Fone Zone's path towards a national identity. But the case for buying Next Byte went further than just that.

Selling a mobile phone is a consultative sale, a bit like a slow dance. You pick a retailer and show a bit of interest. They show a lot of interest back, listening to your needs and your reasons for wanting a mobile. They want you to hang around, stay longer, and will target the phone they believe best fulfils your needs. It's not rocket science, but it is different from the purchase of a pair of jeans where you might see them in a window, like them and buy them immediately. A mobile phone sale might take 40 minutes and the sale is not the end game; it's using the device as a conduit to sell an array of other items that makes the purchase attractive to the retailer. It's the same with computing, and Fone Zone believed that Next Byte offered a selling synergy. It ticked a second box.

The third box the purchase ticked aligned with the industry analysts' belief that mobility and computing would soon converge. 'We anticipated that smart phones and tablets were coming and we wanted to take advantage of that convergence of product from computing to mobility,' Maxine says. Smart phones and computers would morph largely into the same item and would be able to interact autonomously and be used as a one-stop shop for information, education and entertainment. With the third box ticked, Fone Zone wrote out a cheque and the deal with Next Byte was done.

Those three reasons were all valid motivations and at this point it seemed a wise move. But context, and an ability to read the market, is crucial in any strategy. Did Fone Zone need Next Byte to achieve the goals, represented by the ticked boxes? Would convergence have happened anyway? Would Apple products have become more available in Australia through other channels? What were the values of the owners? What was their culture? Why were they so keen to sell? These were the questions Maxine now wishes she had asked.

'Hindsight is a wonderful thing,' Vita Group legal counsel and company secretary Mark Anning says. 'We can beat ourselves up about decisions made in the past, but to be fair to ourselves, at the time we weren't aware – and I doubt the people we were dealing with at Apple were aware – that they would, within a couple of years, have a significant online presence and open stores in direct competition with our own stores.'

Apple's move into Australia kneecapped the part of the strategy that made Next Byte more important in the market place as the primary authorised Apple dealer. That meant nothing when Apple itself was a player.

A lack of due diligence raised another issue soon after the purchase went ahead in 2007: the numbers didn't quite stack up. Apple was growing and that made Fone Zone's purchase look both timely and strategic – but the markups on products at retail were minuscule because the Apple model captured the margins upstream of Australia. This point became obvious quickly, and as anyone in business knows, when you have low margins, it makes it very difficult to invest.

It's important to consider the relationship between the executive team and the board, which also plays a role in due diligence. Maxine offers a mea culpa here. 'We probably didn't allow the board to do its job. There were heated discussions over price and whether enough due diligence had been done. But a wife will always back her husband – and the other way round – over others, and that's been another lesson here too.'

It wasn't long before the whole foundation of Fone Zone's decision to buy Next Byte started to look flaky. Sure, Fone Zone acquired the biggest Apple reseller in Australia – but the decision by Apple to control its own brands and open its own stores immediately hurt Next Byte's dominant market position. The geography that they pulled customers from was unprecedented in retail and that was magnified by Apple's decision to sell into mass retailers.

The bottom line is this: the purchase of Next Byte

looked good on paper. Strategically, it even ticked all the boxes. And while hindsight can provide valuable insight, several questions might have stopped the sale going ahead. Context wasn't considered enough. Neither was an assessment of the looming tech landscape, or Apple's margin model. By mid-December 2015, Vita made the decision to close its Next Byte business.

But herein lies another lesson. Leadership talks regularly refer back to Martin Luther King Jr and his declaration that 'the ultimate measure of a man is not where he stands in moments of comfort and convenience, but where he stands at times of challenge and controversy'. Next Byte's closure showed how Maxine had grown into one of the nation's most successful CEOs. The way she dealt with the situation – both inside and outside the company – proved flawless and evidenced sound behind-the-scenes planning. For several years, Maxine and her leadership team looked at ways of making Next Byte work. But it was obvious that it could not be sustainable in the long term, and the tough decision was eventually made. That decision was black and white; it was the only option. But options existed in when it would be closed and how that should happen, and a cross-functional team was set up to plot the best path forward.

From a business point of view, it would have been foolish to close the Next Byte doors in the lead-up to Christmas, its peak retail period. 'But that worried me,' Maxine says, 'because team members were preparing personally for Christmas and would be committing themselves to debt, hiking up their credit cards without the knowledge held by the leadership team.' Landlords would also be left in the lurch, with vacant sites during the Christmas rush. Maxine knew she had a responsibility to be upfront and share her decision. She told her staff before Christmas. 'We told them what would happen. We told them we had a plan to deploy as many people as we could, and we had support on hand for those we couldn't re-deploy. We kept everyone in the loop at each step,' she says. 'We treated them with respect. We didn't try and deceive them. It was an upsetting thing to do. I felt as though I had failed them.' Christmas celebrations in 2015 were suitably muted.

Next Byte's purchase and closure yielded significant lessons. 'It really was a huge and hard thing to learn,' Maxine says. 'It was a multi-million dollar transaction and we do stronger due diligence now on a $2 million transaction than we did on the Next Byte acquisition. There were a number of things that we should have picked up and we didn't. We also didn't have the right experts at that time in the business to provide that advice.'

Maxine says companies should allow for a 'gut feel factor' when it comes to large transactions. She knows the purchase would not have gone ahead if she had pursued the answers to the questions posed above. She says she regrets not visiting the stores and the service departments and spending one-on-one time with the senior leaders. 'Maybe it's a woman's intuition or that gut instinct I sometimes talk about but in my heart I knew it was not right and I should have been more involved with David during negotiations.' She allowed others to make the decision and didn't question them sufficiently. 'I suppose I can say anything now, but it really was, all along, a crucial strategic failure which I shouldn't have allowed to happen.'

It wasn't that Maxine and David were not strategic. The decision to raise private equity and to embark on a path of acquisition over organic growth was proof of that; a good strategy that worked in principle. They also identified early that the industry was consolidating so their path to growth was not all directed at greenfield sites.

'We switched to acquisition and developed a strong three-year plan that was about picking the best of the industry,' Maxine says. 'The strategy to get private equity was so that we had money for acquisitions. Up until that point we were paying ourselves a very small salary, ploughing everything else back into the business and growing organically. We sold a share of the company for $8 million but we knew that when private equity comes into the business it stays for between three and five years – and the main avenue to exit is through an IPO. That decision to float was crucial for us to reach the next step.'

Maxine mentions those decisions as examples of well-considered strategy. 'Those were big strategies, carefully crafted, then along comes Next Byte and we made that decision which on the surface fitted our strategy but certainly didn't underneath.'

Maxine says the episode also taught her that any mistake is compounded if it is not addressed quickly. 'I think ego got in the way and I think we kept saying, "No, this is a great thing". We kept ploughing on and on but the model was flawed. We were unwilling to admit that we had made a mistake.'

She says admitting mistakes is always harder when it's company, not private, money involved. Ensuring any new acquisition fits the culture of your existing business is important too, and Next Byte struggled alongside Fone Zone prompting a name change, in April 2008, from Fone Zone Group Limited to Vita (Italian for 'way of life') Group Limited.

The Australian Institute of Company Directors says that good strategy involves 'a clear and specific statement of goals, one that is challenging, yet achievable and grounded in the context of the organisation's environment as well as a clear statement of how the organisation intends to achieve those goals'. *The First XI*, a study of leading businesses in Australia, charts successful strategy in steps: focused regional development, then geographic spread and related expansion, experiment with diversification (or international expansion), then consolidation.

In recent years, Vita Group's strategy has mirrored both the AICD guidance and the paths followed by some of Australia's top companies. The 2009 licence agreement with Telstra, which saw Fone Zone grow to own and operate about 25 per cent of the carrier's stores nationwide, is a case in point. But the lessons that came out of Next Byte will live with Maxine for a long time. Strategy used to be over the breakfast table with her husband. Then it became an articulated annual plan. Now it's an all-inclusive process that sits within the cultural framework of the company. Looking to the future, Vita Group plans to continue working on its retail channels to drive high returns, but it will focus on the small to medium business market to capitalise on growth opportunities there. Enterprise and government customers are also a key part of Vita Group's strategy, where opportunity lies in duplicating the success gained in retail.

'You still summarise it once a year and we budget the year financially on it, but we are continually looking at the business,' Maxine says. So is her leadership team, but Maxine sees her main role as keeping the business on strategy. 'That's the job of the CEO. I repeatedly ask people whether a decision is on strategy.' If they argue that it's not but could be worth pursuing, she is adamant. 'There are no buts – unless it's on that strategy document I don't want to talk about it because it is wasting everybody's time.' That's not to say a quality strategy is inflexible. 'You need to make sure your team is with you, and if something is not working, it needs to be addressed. But that's common sense. In fact, there is no shame in getting the strategy wrong. The wrong thing is not identifying it and fixing it. Next Byte had to close. We didn't have an option, but I could not be more proud of the way that closure was handled: a hard decision was taken, we worked together strategically, and with our values at the heart of what we decided, we re-deployed team members where we could, and treated everyone in a respectful manner. The lesson I've learnt along the way is: "It's not what you do … it's how you do it."'

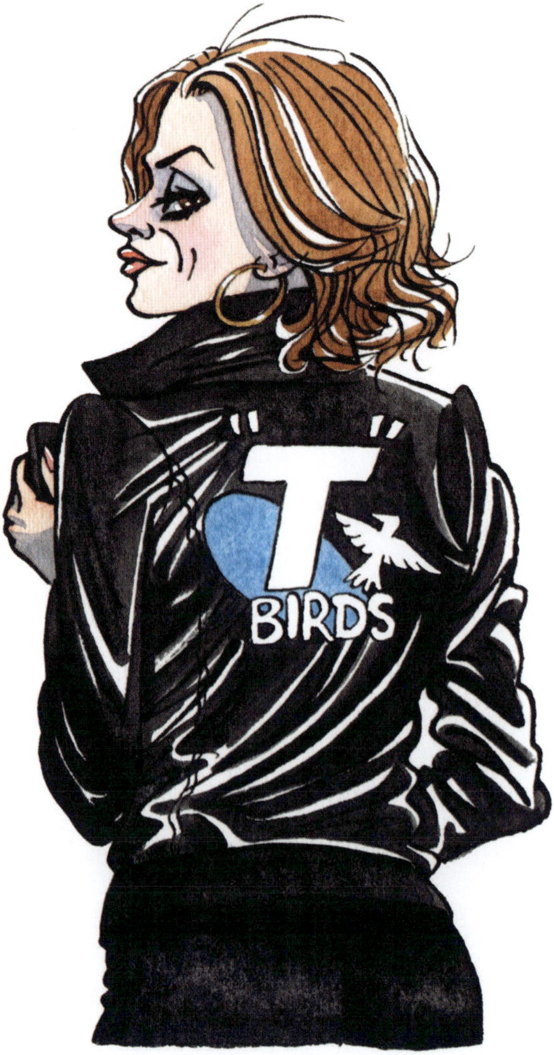
"T"
BIRDS

4.

Stand and Deliver

'However beautiful the strategy, you should occasionally look at the results.' – Sir Winston Churchill, former British Prime Minister

Sometimes you get it right first up. In a book of business lessons, it's important to celebrate that. Business brings unexpected good times where revenue rushes in through the door and profits shoot for the stars. More often than not, though, it presents unrelenting challenges. Maxine pinpoints one instance – where her team rolled out 85 Telstra stores in just over three years – as an example where everything that could work, did work. It remains a shining example of what can be achieved when meticulous planning, know-how and cohesive teamwork come together.

Many small businesses have opened a retail outlet and know the detailed checklist that needs to be developed and implemented in a specific order: from lease negotiations, to fit-out, IT, recruitment and marketing. It is a Herculean task, where each step needs to fit neatly with the one before it. 'Operation Grease' was the name given to the project to roll out 100 stores. It was a sound strategy that provided the company with a new income stream. But it wasn't the strategy that made it work; it was how it was implemented.

'Having a strategy is important – but the execution of it actually rates higher,' Maxine says. 'You can have the best strategy in the world, but if you don't execute it, it's worthless.'

At the heart of the national roll-out was the licence agreement which was signed by Vita Group and Telstra in 2009. Maxine had been a Telstra dealer for almost 15 years, but this agreement set a precedent where Vita Group could now open and operate up to 100 Telstra stores and a number of Telstra business centres for its small to medium business customers. Telstra had 370 stores Australia-wide, but not all of them were owned or run by Telstra. It was Telstra's aim that customers wouldn't know the owner of the store because they would be consistently branded and operated, all reflecting the same high quality.

In fact, Telstra owned only 89 stores; independent licensees, often termed 'mum and dad operators' held 181; and the new licence agreement allowed Maxine, who had a handful of stores (in addition to her own 146 Fone Zone-branded retail outlets) to increase her holding up to 100 Telstra stores. The remuneration model meant Vita Group received a one-off fee and payments for high levels of customer service. Now it is broadly based on a mix of volumes sold, types of product offered and customer advocacy levels.

Before explaining the roll-out, it is important to understand why this strategy of transformation was important. Like many companies, Vita Group emerged from the global financial crisis with an eye on the new economy and what might be around the corner. Two trends stood out: firstly, a market shift was occurring where the high end of town was doing well, as was the bottom end. But Fone Zone sat squarely in the middle, and that was a concern. Secondly, there was another factor at play. One response to the uncertainty resulting from the global financial crisis was a reversion to trusted brands. Apple was one example but across the board customers were embracing brands and leaving non-specific branded retailers in their wake. For instance, coffee lovers looked to buy their own Nespresso machine, while big retailers who stocked high-end fashion lost customers to outlets run by those fashion houses. At the bottom end, customers flocked to $2 shops for everything from costumes to stationery.

Vita Group board chair Dick Simpson says branded stores offered more expansive ranges than non-specific retailers, and customers followed the brands. This meant that non-branded stores dropped their prices. He says they could see the traffic in Telstra, Optus and Vodafone branded stores and knew they needed to act. 'It was from the realisation that the world was going branded that we thought – okay, we better do something about it.'

Maxine says the company's inability to 'yell product and price' meant it would have been silly to acquire other product and price businesses. 'It wasn't in our DNA,' she says. 'We knew how to be service-focused and so we looked at the points of presence here in Australia for Telstra, Vodafone and Optus.'

Telstra was under-represented in shops. Vita Group, at this stage, only had a handful of Telstra stores, as an independent licensee, and 146 Fone Zone stores. It realised that the Telstra brand would attract more customers and combined with the proven customer service capability in Fone Zone it would be a winning formula.

'We knew that we had to move from Fone Zone to Telstra ... but in negotiating that deal, we signed ourselves up to some pretty stiff targets: rolling out 25 stores a year,' Maxine says. 'In addition to that, we had to come out of the one brand and into another. We had to keep everybody in the business on track and if we hadn't executed that well, we would probably have lost the business in 12 months.'

Inside Telstra, similar conversations were occurring. John Boniciolli ran all Telstra's non-branded channels, including Fone Zone in 2008. He knew the market was changing, not only because of that shift towards brands and the question mark over non-telco specialist retailers, but because digital changes and a new market competitiveness were adding variables to the equation. He says two likely scenarios stood out to him.

'One was to take [the relationship between Telstra and Fone Zone] to a complete level of partnership, akin to a licence agreement. The other thing was this: if we can't make that work, we'll face a gradual decline,' he says. 'I didn't know at that time if we could make it work – but I had enough respect for Fone Zone and Maxine to give it a go.'

Both organisations brought in an international strategic consulting firm to help find a path that would provide a new stream of growth. In the end, the options were clear. Fone Zone, being a non-branded retailer, would suffer if it continued on its current trajectory. Maxine and David knew that, and so did Telstra. But Telstra stood to gain by reworking its relationship with Vita Group too. This is because while sentiment was sending customers into its branded outlets, it needed to increase the number of outlets fast, and ensure a value set that comprehensively mirrored its own.

It was an emotional pull for Maxine. This was her company. She'd almost lost it in 1996 through a partnership with Interact (those events are detailed in

Chapter 13). Then she could have lost it again in the global financial crisis. Now, its future growth was being stymied and the best path ahead removed the brand she had built and replaced it with Telstra.

She knew it was the way forward, though. Within Vita Group, they had tried to drive the Fone Zone business harder, but that proved difficult when customer numbers were declining. Having learnt to look to other markets, Maxine realised the writing was on the wall; across the globe, telco carriers were starting to take over the ownership of their channels. It was happening in Australia and she couldn't see that changing.

The licence agreement which was recommended by the strategic consulting firms built on rather than changed the relationship between Vita Group and Telstra. Both organisations became more crucial to each other. The negotiations, and the bumpy ride that went with them, are dealt with elsewhere in this book, but the marathon deliberations cemented the relationship. Telstra wanted to increase its national footprint via more points of presence, and it wanted its brand to be more prominent in the marketplace. Vita Group wanted to survive and prosper. In between, negotiation was waged over customer service, targeting particular customer segments, team member capability and in-store conversion. After months of negotiation the licence agreement was signed, providing the Vita Group with a way forward with a premium partner.

CEOs and boards often talk about the crucial role

of strategy. But Maxine's view is that strategy comes second to successful implementation. Her point, made earlier, is that it is fruitless to dream up the world's best plan and not be able to execute it. It's far better to have a workman-like strategy that is rolled out beautifully. The licence agreement, in any judgement, was a shining example of a successful strategy. But Maxine's focus was on how it was rolled out. Otherwise, it would be useless.

'Execution is harder in many ways because three people can sit down and work out a strategy. Execution involves all of the business working together,' she says.

The name 'Operation Grease' came from the classic American film – a pointer to the quirkiness that characterises Vita Group's culture. Inside Vita Group Telstra was called the big T, reminding Maxine of the T-Birds headed by Danny who played opposite the Pink Ladies. That was the easy decision; those that followed were more nuanced, complex and protracted. 'We spent a lot of time talking,' Maxine says. Her project team, which was led by project manager Tracie McLauchlan, calls it 'swimming laps'. It was at these planning meetings that every single minute job involved in rolling out a new store was articulated and given to someone as their assigned task. Communication was key. 'We told everyone what we were doing, why we were doing it and what their role in it was. We spent a lot of time on that.'

The list of required jobs – which numbered more than 120 for each store – was then slotted into a gated approach so that the order flowed properly, and so that no step was taken before the one before it was completed.

'The gated process was crucial,' Maxine says. 'It's okay when you are opening one store – but we were opening one a week. It's also about a 20-week process from negotiation over a site to opening the store. You go down the list – from looking at the legal issues to shop-fitting and design, to ordering chairs, recruitment, training, ordering stock ... Few people probably realise how many different jobs are required for one store to open its doors.'

Mistakes were made along the way, but nothing major. 'If we missed anything, it would then be fed into the gated process and captured the next time,' Maxine says. All the listed jobs fell into big bucket headings such as lease negotiations, design, build, recruitment, operational and learning. Over time, the aim was that the 'learning' category grew smaller and smaller, and it did. All jobs were marked red, until completed, when they were slotted to green. Each gated process had a representative from every department in the building, and that team would meet weekly. All the details were gathered and could be viewed on a shared computer drive.

'If you were allocated a specific task, you had to do that and then it was your responsibility to go in and change it from red to green,' Maxine says. That meant that the weekly meetings were short; they only ever addressed issues still marked red. 'We managed our business by exception; don't look at what's already been done – focus on the jobs that still need to be done.'

The roll-out covered every State in Australia and ran from 2009 until 2013. 'I remember sitting across table from investors and analysts saying what we were going to do and you could just see the doubt on their faces,' Maxine says. 'I have great delight now going back and saying, "I told you so!".' One complicating factor was the role of Fone Zone, which still owned and operated 146 stores. 'We had to keep those stores generating profits to fund the roll-out.'

Team members were not chosen on their seniority, or even their experience. 'They were chosen because they were the doers and could do what needed to be done,' Maxine says. That's an important tip when it comes to picking a team. Too many leaders can be a bit like too many cooks in the kitchen. Staff who regularly ordered the stationery, or checked the business names on the registers, or ensured that the cheque went to the lawyer on time were included. 'If you don't do those smaller things there are delays and that can impact the whole project,' Maxine says.

While the intention was to roll out 100 stores, the plan halted at 85. 'I was cognizant of the fact that if we kept opening greenfields, at some point we would have to close some of them – so I thought we should stop, sweat our assets and then regroup again,' Maxine says.

What would she do differently if the same project ran again? 'Not much,' she says. 'It wasn't a lesson I had to learn this time but communication is absolutely crucial. My advice is that if you think you've communicated something well, go and communicate it again. You cannot over-communicate. People need to know why they are doing something, what the strategy is behind it, what their role in it is, and what happens if they don't do it. I really struggle with the notion that some business leaders hide so much from their teams. You are all in it together and someone down the chain can hamper progress if they don't understand the mission and its goals.'

Pete Connors says the roll-out galvanised the company and provided a strong road forward. He worked with Telstra to determine where stores would be located and then, taking his CEO's advice, he would get on a plane and go and watch consumers in the local district.

The role of the 'ant trail' in Vita Group's success is chronicled in other parts of this book, but in brief, Maxine believes you maximise your customer visits if you open your store along the line where customers follow each other from the car park around the shopping centre. Often it ends at a big department store or a grocery store. To be stationed near either of those would always prove fruitful. Pete Connors would visit the site, sit down and watch where the ant trail went. Where did customers park? What entry into the shopping centre did they use? What direction did they then go? He knew that rents might have been higher there, but it would be repaid time and time again through customer support.

Bell Potter securities director - equities Cyril Jinks first met Maxine at an investor briefing in 2009. An industrial stock investor, Jinks was looking at different sectors when he was drawn to Vita Group, even though its share price had been up and down over the years, going as low as seven cents and breaking the $1 mark at the other end.

'Maxine spoke with such intensity and passion and knew every bit of the detail,' Jinks says now. 'She told me she had been waiting for an opportunity [like the licence agreement] for five years.' Jinks says Maxine's great strength, which shows in its profits, was to get the Vita Group culture infused across all stores quickly. 'That's a real skill,' he says. 'She's not some romantic businesswoman. What I saw in Maxine was high energy, determination and an unbelievable commitment.'

In Maxine's Words

'The collective wisdom and effort of the team always outperforms the individual. That never used to be a value, but it became one as we were going through Operation Grease. You cannot over-communicate in a business, because if you don't tell people what's happening, they'll make up their own rubbish and their own rubbish is way worse than what's really happening. That's why I have this policy that anyone can call me. Operation Grease was a really important project that we executed well and with speed and we still run today. It also demonstrated to Telstra what our value was. Before that we were providing volume, but then they could see the depth of what we do. It showcased quality communication and collaboration. It was a very clear of example of what you can achieve when you think smart and run hard.'

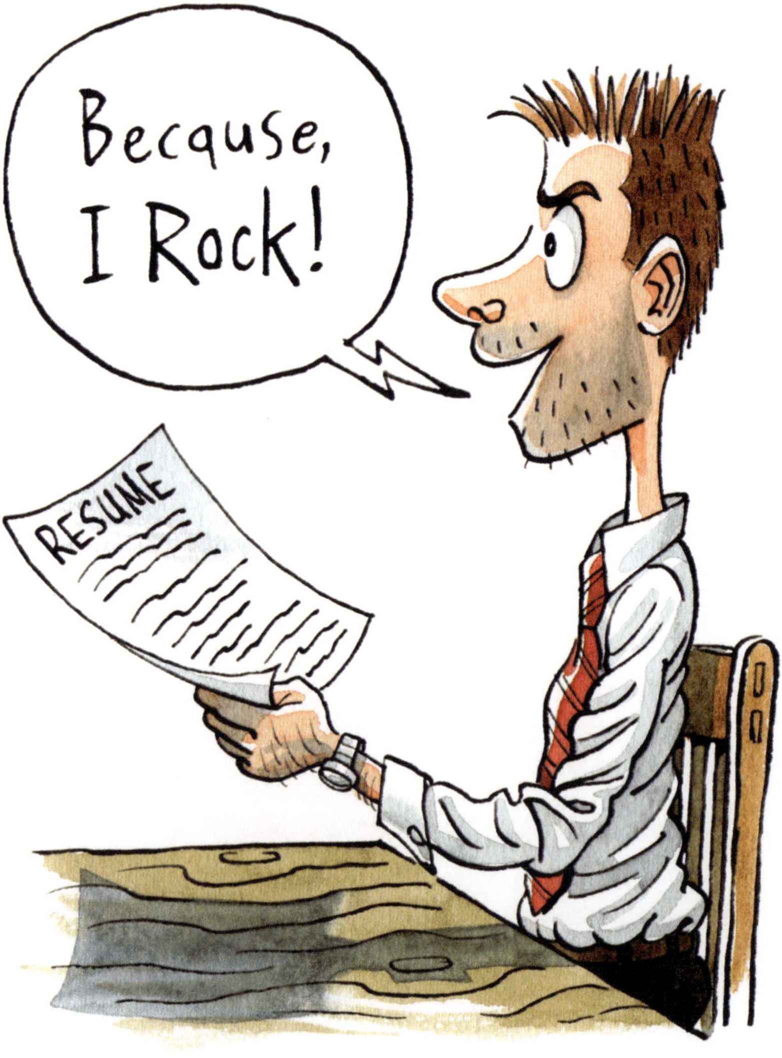
Because,
I Rock!
RESUME

5.

Employ for Will Not Skill

'The basic idea that incentives can be used to motivate behaviour is a powerful one. It works for employees and it has a clear place in parenting as anyone who has tried to potty train a recalcitrant toddler with sticker rewards knows.' – American economist Emily Oster

Ben Johnson was working at McDonald's on Queensland's Sunshine Coast in 2002 when a mate told him about an opening for a local Fone Zone store manager. Johnson went home and applied immediately and managed to score an interview. Not long after, he arrived early at the company's support centre in Eagle Farm, an industrial suburb nine kilometres from Brisbane's CBD. He couldn't put his finger on it immediately, but the support centre was unlike any office he had ever seen. It wasn't just that it was located geographically in a place that looked out of kilter, but inside its shell it didn't resemble any office that came to mind.

People were busy, rushing about, dressed more for fun than work. A woman stood at the centre, giving orders, but in a very casual way. She seemed to be the boss, but didn't quite fit with his expectations. Young, with a touch of schoolboy arrogance, Johnson didn't think it would be that woman, Maxine Horne, who would decide his future. 'I thought, surely she's not going to interview me,' he says now. 'And she did. I reckon I was the first in a long time to render her speechless.'

Johnson sat across the table from Maxine and answered her questions. They were unusual too, and few related to his work history. What did he like to do? What did he find difficult to do? What was the biggest challenge he'd faced so far? Tell me something about yourself? The questions all bordered on the personal. That intrigued him and he enjoyed sitting back and honestly responding. He didn't know where he got the answer to the last question, but it worked.

'Tell me,' Maxine said. 'Why should you get this job?'

Johnson didn't hesitate. 'Because I rock.'

With those words, the job indeed was his.

'I laughed,' Maxine says now, 'and walked away

thinking that I had to employ him because I like that attitude. I always employ for will, never skill. Skill is not important to me at that point. I can teach someone how to become skilled at what they need to do here but I don't know anyone who can teach someone to have the will to do it. They have to bring that with them when they walk through the door.'

Ben Johnson certainly did and quickly became one of Fone Zone's star employees, beginning as store manager at Kawana Waters on Queensland's Sunshine Coast, before transferring across to the company's marketing department, and moving up to the position of marketing manager. Throughout that journey, his relationship with Maxine Horne mirrored that original interview in which she probed him on his personal decision-making ability. She expected absolute will; she provided the training for skill. And, unlike most employers, she remained on top of his personal life too.

'She took a mentoring role and told me to pull my head in at different times but I also remember a conversation we had at the beginning. She said people would always leave the company with more skills than they brought to it. I did and I'll always remember that.'

That personal mentoring role – a hallmark of how Maxine operates – runs through the business. It's in her DNA. 'We often say it's about working your personal brand,' she says. 'What you say or do – it's all about your personal brand.' In her view, that gives her the right to pull up an employee drinking too much at a function, or have a fireside chat with someone whose behaviour is affecting others or their work. Across the organisation, several young team members have had that chat about how they act after hours and how that reflects on their 'brand'. It seems to be accepted, even appreciated.

'The biggest sense of pride that I get is watching people go through the organisation,' Maxine says. Her determination to choose applicants on will means she has stayed on interview panels much longer than she would have otherwise. 'For me, it's a can-do attitude. They want to better themselves, so they have set personal goals. That could be a rock climb or it could be something else – but it shows me that they are goal-oriented and driven.' It also opens the company up to a wider pool of potential applicants, because not having the skills to perform a job at the outset does not prohibit someone from winning the job. 'Just because a young person is studying for medicine at university doesn't mean he or she can't use those brains in our organisation for four years. I'm not sure why every business doesn't do that.'

Maxine says she has never asked an employee to do something she would not do. When she visits a store, particularly before the company's national footprint got so big, she'd greet customers, talk with them, and sell them their mobile phone. She'd sweep the store if it needed to be done, and has since travelled through each department, on each floor, to understand the task and to show those doing it on a daily basis that she was prepared to do it.

Maxine highlights how important will is with a story from the opening of the first Fone Zone store on the Gold Coast in January 1995.

'We took over this toy store that had gone bust and the outside was a turret of a castle,' she says. With a newly-minted deal with Telstra, it was being painted blue and orange. 'We went in without a lot of know-how. The day we opened, there were no landlines available. I painted it in a gloss and of course the paint was still wet when customers walked through the doors – and when they walked out again. They'd put their hands down or brush up against the wall and they'd have all this paint over them.' The point of this story is not her strategic thinking, or her ability to plan. 'This is why I focus so much on will, not skill,' she says. 'I didn't have the skill to prevent that from happening, but I had the will to fix it. I ran off to the local hardware store and got rags and turpentine. I stood at the door as people were leaving and would say, "Can I just wipe that off you?" – and their hands would end up smelling worse! The point is that I had the will to fix it. I could have chosen to ignore it, but instead I tried really hard to resolve it. Did I solve the problem entirely? No. But the fact that I wanted to help enabled them to empathise with me and it became funny. It's will that drives it and it's the basis of good customer service.'

Twelve years after Ben Johnson was offered a job at Fone Zone, Maxine sat across a table from him at a company dinner. 'You know what, Ben?' she said, leaning closer. 'It's probably time that you moved on and got some experience somewhere else.'

Johnson remembers those words like it was yesterday. 'I was gutted, absolutely gutted,' he says now. 'I'd given her a third of my life and she was ending it.' Maxine thought he was good at his job; invaluable even. But she had taught him to the point where he wasn't learning as much as he might elsewhere. It was time for her to let go and for him to move on. Johnson knows it was the right decision. 'In hindsight it really was the right thing to do. It was one of those tough love things.'

There are many other employees who Maxine has hired for will and then, when they have reached a point, she's taken them aside and suggested they continue their career trajectory elsewhere. 'They haven't lost the will, but I've provided all the skill I can – and I'm happy to see them go and grow,' she says. But it's never easy, as any employer knows. 'It's a shitty conversation to have. I just make sure that no-one else does it, and no-one else should do it.' And during that conversation, Maxine reminds them of the promise she made on their first day. 'They will always leave the company with more skills than they arrived, and I make sure that is always the case.'

It's not only the 'will not skill' mantra that you hear repeated by Vita Group's leadership team. Two others go to the heart of the company's employment strategy and the way 'team members' play a part in the organisation. The first is a company responsibility, in Maxine's view, to provide each employee with 'purpose, mastery and autonomy'. 'Purpose' ensures everybody understands why they are doing a task. 'When I talk about the purpose, it really is about sharing the vision,' Maxine says. 'This is where we, as a business, are going and this is how we are going to get there, and this your role to play in it.' Maxine says that provides all employees with a contextual picture, and their role in painting that landscape. 'And I tell them why. I take the company's vision – the company's purpose – and make it theirs. They then know their task is to focus on their role. If every single person in the organisation does that, we'll achieve the end goal.'

'Mastery' goes back to providing the skill for those with the will to learn. Once the team member knows their task, they are trained and coached so that they can reach a level of 'mastery'. The final part of the equation is providing employees with the 'autonomy' they need to do, and grow, in the job; a mistake employers often make, according to Maxine. This is because they provide the purpose and mastery, and then 'put the employee in such a straitjacket that they find it hard to feel they have accomplished anything'. They don't value or understand the benefits that flow from autonomy. 'You have to be able to give people the environment to use the skills you have taught them,' she says. 'They need to have that autonomy.'

To cap it off, and to ensure it works, a reward and recognition program is also necessary. Vita Group spends pots of money on KPI metrics and more than $1 million annually on a recognition and reward program for consistently high achievers.

Peter F. Drucker, the late Harvard Business School professor regarded as a guru of modern management theory, says the best management decisions come from putting the right people into the right jobs. 'The soldier has a right to competent command was already an old maxim at the time of Julius Caesar,' he wrote in the *Harvard Business Review* in 1985. 'It is the duty of managers to make sure that the responsible people in their organisations perform.' How best to do this? 'Making the right people decisions is the ultimate means of controlling an organisation well. Such decisions reveal how competent management is, what its values are and whether it takes its job seriously.'

Maxine's recruitment and training strategies are underpinned by the belief that 80 per cent of people sit in the middle of an organisation, wedged between the 10 per cent of high achievers and the 10 per cent of low achievers. By lifting the performance of that big centre chunk, the organisation can lift its performance, and its bottom line. That view is not new and indeed parallels to it have existed in parts of the education sector for years. Many tutorial schools make their profits by encouraging parents to believe their child's report card could improve with the right help. A pass can become a credit; a credit move closer to a distinction. That makes sense. Some students, no matter what amount of coaching, might remain at the bottom of the class academically. That's not to say they won't shine in other ways, but it might not be the priority other activities are to them. Another cohort will always sit in the top 10 per cent; perhaps they work harder, or are blessed with a natural intelligence, or are more competitive than their peers. A teacher's effort, with both those cohorts is probably limited; perhaps he or she can lift the bottom 10 per cent or the top 10 per cent a smidgeon. But if that big middle cohort can move five per cent, the lift in class average will be significant.

Maxine sees sales in the same way. The high-end sales teams are self-motivated go-getters who exhibit enormous self-discipline and are driven either by success, or fear of failure. She can't influence them too much, apart from providing the environment to do well and the recognition and rewards that accompany that success. At the other end, there will be those who consistently are unable to convert a chat to a sale. Maybe they lack the personality required, or the discipline, or even the preparedness to learn. That remains the case, irrespective of the coaching provided to them.

Maybe, Maxine says, they're not cut out for a job in sales. 'They aren't prepared for the nine times someone will say "no" that they have to take in order to get the one "yes",' she says. 'Sales is a numbers game – no matter what you do, 10 per cent will over-perform and 10 per cent will under-perform. In the middle is the bulk of your team and it's just a simple maths. If you move that group by five per cent towards the top, you've managed a huge improvement. But what happens is, and I have seen it time and time again, businesses overload the top performers and move them to a position where they are making it difficult for them to learn, or they are ignoring them. The top performers need attention, but a different kind of attention. My advice is do not ignore that big middle ground where a difference can really be made.'

Maxine has always walked into an interview room with a plan, and it continues with any appointment to her leadership team now. She wants to know whether the applicant is able to set goals and achieve them. That means personal questions. She's looking for them to say that they wanted to run a marathon, or visit some faraway destination, or take up quilting. She doesn't care too much what the goal is, or even whether the applicant has reached that goal yet. The answer needs to address the steps the applicant is taking in order to meet it.

'That shows me how they think, their process in trying to achieve something and their level of discipline,' she says. 'That provides a very good picture of someone's personality.' The second part of the interview looks at resilience, and the questions will relate to some adversity or challenge they have been forced to overcome. 'That tells me whether they will give up. Life isn't ever presented on a plate. You need to be able to deal with adversities and that's why I go down that line of questioning.' Next, she turns to the empathy of the applicant. That used to be addressed, solely, by questions, but in recent years, as in most big companies, it has grown more complex and targeted. 'When we bring someone in, they get a psychological test and we test their emotional intelligence,' she says. 'It's really, really important because work is just a component of someone's life, and whether we like it or not, if we are a good leader we will get involved with people's personal lives. It's not that we are intrusive, but they will come to work and be upset and you will notice it because that is what good leaders do. And a good leader will say, "Hey, I'm here if you want to talk about it because you don't seem right" or, "Why don't you go and get yourself a coffee because something has rattled you this morning?". Those are the things that I really look for when I'm interviewing because there needs to be a cultural fit, and if there's not, it's never going to work.'

In Maxine's Words

'There are two reasons why people don't do things: one is skill and the other is will. Skilling an employee is my job and the organisation's job. We have to be able to teach someone how to do something. That's very different to will – and there's nothing I can do about someone's will. Our average entry age is 22. That means for 22 years, someone has been indoctrinated. I'm not going to change much in three years, so I need to find out, before employing them, whether they are prepared to learn. Do they like learning? Do they want to become a better person – and that doesn't just mean achieving better sales. Are they respectful? When I look at resumés, I search for whether they have been in teams, because everything we do is team-based. Yes, we have individual salespeople, but we operate as part of a team. At interviews, I ask about the really bad times they've had and how they felt about that –

particularly if they're applying for a leadership role. And I ask them whether they've ever had to let someone go. If they say "yes", I ask them to talk me through it, and they'll normally explain how they weren't doing their job and they had to act. That's not what I mean. I love that quote of Maya Angelou: "At the end of the day people won't remember what you said or did, they will remember how you made them feel." That's why I go down that line of questioning. I want to understand how it made them feel, what makes them tick, how resilient they are. Their answers guide me on whether they will fit in, culturally, here.'

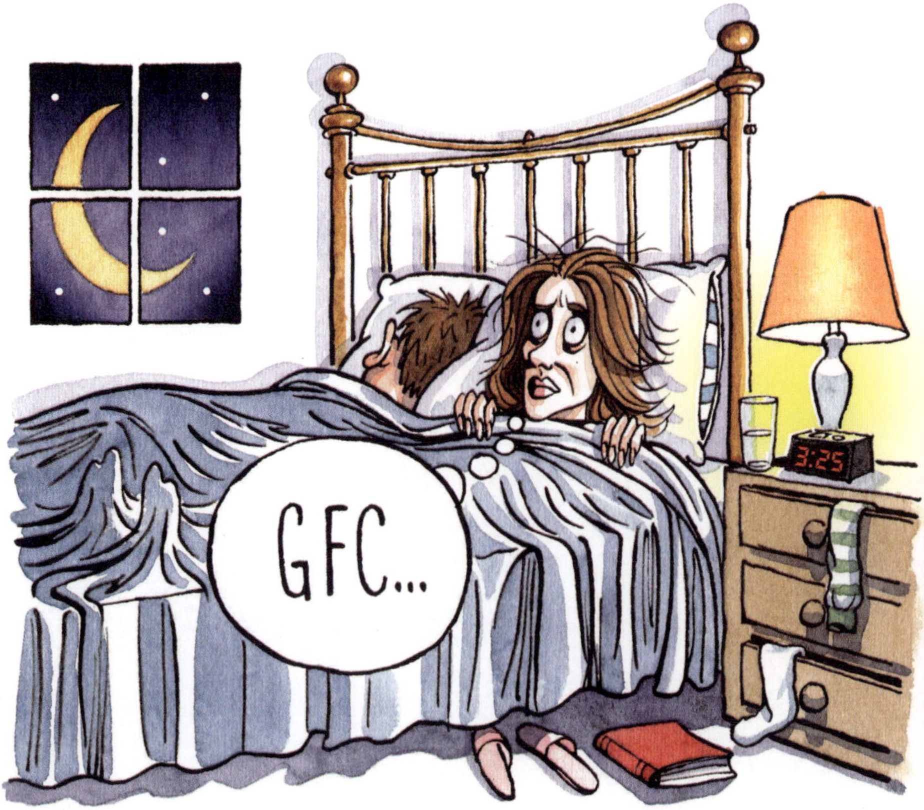
GFC...
3:25

6.

Look After Your Own

'Treat employees like partners and they act like partners.'
– American comedian Fred Allen

The global financial crisis (GFC) of 2007–08 bore down heavily on small business, forcing it to squeeze every bit out of each dollar invested. Headlines chronicled the threat it posed to our big financial institutions and the government's responses to that. But the economic shenanigans had even wider effects: housing markets suffered, unemployment rose, consumer confidence plummeted. Many businesses went to the wall. Others dug deep into rainy day reserves just to stay afloat. Almost everyone learnt some kind of lesson and Fone Zone was no different. Indeed, it felt buffeted up against the economic story on one side and being caught out by the pace of technological change on the other. In particular, the Next G network with its increased capacity came online more quickly than anyone expected, catching manufacturers unaware and leaving retailers with insufficient stock of handsets for customers wanting the latest.

The combination of economic uncertainty and a will to wait for the best and latest slowed sales. Overnight, in early 2007, sales volumes halved. The share price joined others in a downhill slide and Maxine and David started looking at ways to save. Stores were re-rostered and run on lean staff levels. The P&L was combed for every spare bit of fat. Maxine lay awake at night, wondering whether the business they'd built from scratch, the business she had poured most waking hours into, would go belly-up like so many others. Daylight, though, hardened her resolve to trade through the bad news. It would be better on the other side.

'We were overstaffed and learnt that it is important to continually look at the expense base,' she says. 'Don't only look when you are forced to.' She gives, as an example, a recent flurry of emails from team members in one area happy to take on more work. 'I had a sense we have a little bit of slack and you only need a little downturn for that to translate into laying people off.' That means contract employment has become more valuable, so that the ability to be flexible is greater.

'Employing somebody is an obligation. You have a responsibility to see that through and I'd hate to be in a position where you employ somebody and six months later you are making them redundant. I think that shows bad foresight and preparation. If I'm honest, we had got a little bit lazy in 2007 and 2008 and we let the business get fat. I think people expected us to make people redundant. A lot of businesses were doing that. What our team members didn't expect was our decision to pull our customer service programs.'

This is the key lesson learnt by Maxine during the GFC. Faced with a declining share price, an economy that was forcing business to batten the hatches, and a fear that the Vita Group could fail, a decision was made that Maxine regrets to this day.

'We stripped out all the team members' benefits and a lot of the customer service programs, and to this day I wish we hadn't,' she says. But it didn't stop there. Having targeted team member benefits, key components of the company's CARE program – its customer service bible and the point of difference in the industry in Maxine's belief – was pulled too. Together those two decisions saved a few pennies, but prompted heartaches that took years to heal. 'Each morning, in each store, there is a morning meeting; time taken out to think about the day ahead,' Maxine says. 'How will we approach customers today? What are some talking points? What's the thing we're going to address in our personal approach? It's team time; time when each of the team members knows they are being heard.' Even these meetings were curtailed to save a few bucks. Store water coolers were taken out. Coffee vouchers were stopped. Lolly jars were put away. Toys were removed. By themselves, they were small moves – but the decision carried considerable symbolism.

To team members, an irony was playing out; small privileges were being taken away at exactly the same time they were being asked to work harder. The quarterly pow-wow dinners, where business leaders could take their team out and the company would fund it to the tune of $20 a head, went too. Some of the reward and recognition programs, where individuals and teams were given holidays and bonuses for hard work, were halted. In a sales environment, that cruelled enthusiasm.

Maxine knows that now. She also knows that the best sales staff genuinely appreciate recognition; it is a driver of their behaviour. Ripping that out slowed the motivation of many to sell. It meant that some of the sales team didn't strive as hard. Stores, which at the beginning of the GFC boasted small toy zones to entertain children while their parents or carers sought advice, were packed up and put away. Even small pockets of sponsorship in local communities were put on hold. Each of these measures saved a few dollars, but the impact of those decisions lasted several years.

A good example of that is a component of the CARE program which Maxine's own team had authored – the free coffee voucher. When customers enter a retail store they are assigned a salesperson who looks after their needs. Sometimes there is a waiting period until the appropriate person is free. The CARE program directly addressed that. For example, chairs were provided for those customers who had to wait. And they were offered a free cup of tea or coffee. Maxine did a deal with local coffee shops in each of the centres. Customers loved it. But team members did too; it gave them an authority and an ability to manage the customer flow through the store. Maxine knew that every now and again the voucher system was misused. A team member might grab a coffee. But it didn't happen often.

'You can't build your business on two per cent of people,' she says, 'when 98 per cent will always do the right thing. You have to build a model that takes that into consideration because if you put all of these rules and regulations in to stop the two per cent, then you have actually destroyed what you are trying to do. And that's the mistake some businesses make. They shut down something on impulse because a minority might misuse it, rather than focusing on the sales. I knew that was going on but then I went into that financial crisis and I pulled the coffee vouchers. I wish I hadn't. Again, in isolation, it was only something small. But it had empowered employees and then we took that autonomy away from them. And it had a real effect.'

The impact was profound because it came on the back of the decision to strip out several other small privileges. 'It took me a long time to realise that, and it wasn't really until being out on the floor and talking to people and them saying, "Why can't we have the coffee vouchers – it's really good for our customers?" that it dawned on me that we had done such a good job on the values and driving that customer service ethos, that people felt that we were asking them to do a job but tying their hands behind their back. I had taken away one of their tools of trade.' Maxine says team members were more upset at that decision than they were with the decision to make some people redundant. 'They got that we were in the middle of a financial crisis, but they understandably thought that if I'm here, let me do my job properly.'

Maxine says that although she didn't cancel the entire CARE program, she had removed so many components of it she may as well have quashed it completely. 'It was all my fault. We lost customers and we lost good people too. I took away our team members' ability to please customers and in hindsight it was the wrong way to go. I really didn't understand that it was symbolic to them and it was like we had deserted our roots and that we no longer cared.' Maxine returns to this point several times. It is a mistake she won't make again and she urges other businesses to 'think big picture' when confronted with a hurdle; it will make it easier down the track.

'Timing is important too,' she says. This decision to remove the CARE components was taken because of the prevailing circumstances – but so much comes back to how it is done, not when it is done. She gives a more recent example of whether to close a store in

December. 'I've learnt my lesson and decided not to do it then because it would have made people redundant in the lead-up to Christmas. Is $25,000 – the amount we would have saved – going to kill this business?' She answers her own question, 'No. What is most important is that with team members who are likely to be impacted by something like a store closure – that we do the right thing and provide them with as much notice as possible.' She carried forward this lesson when Vita Group decided to close the Next Byte business.

Caring for her team, apart from the lapse during the global financial crisis, has been a hallmark of Maxine's business methodology; no doubt traced back to the fact that at one stage she was working full time with two small children. Indeed, her son Jack was born on 2 January 1995, just two days before the company signed a significant dealership agreement with Telstra. 'The plan was for me to stop work. I lasted six days. It drove me nuts. I just couldn't and I said to David that I needed to go back to work. It was driving him nuts too. He'd come home and I'd be asking about every single little detail. So I came to work and set up a crèche in my office.'

Few mothers escape the challenge of a child who doesn't like sleep, and Maxine was no different with Jack napping, often, for two hours at a time. A swing was installed in her office and once she set it going, Jack would fall asleep quickly. (Later Maxine would learn she wasn't feeding him enough, prompting him to wake up too often.) 'I used to be in my office negotiating with suppliers like Nokia, banging them down on price to get the deal I needed,' she says. A breast pump, spare nappies and a bottle would adorn the desk as Maxine focused on the business at hand. 'I laugh now but I remember asking a couple of businessmen, on occasion, if they could wind the swing up on their way out!' Maxine knows wealth brings both privilege and options. 'I say to women who are working, I've been really fortunate to have the ability to do that. I know most people don't.' But that experience has had an impact on her view of how a workplace should operate; a view that has seen employee benefits become part of the business years before they did in many other companies.

In Maxine's eyes, there are three steps to looking after team members. The first step is to understand them and who they are so that you are able to have conversations with them that relate to their families or their children, or even their children's schooling. The second step is to be open and honest and tell them directly if they are not doing the job expected of them. 'Nine times out of 10, people don't know. People don't turn up to work thinking, "I am going to do a shit job today. No-one does that. We have not created the right environment, systems, processes or leaders for them to perform.' The third step is to allow some of the flexibility that fortune allowed her. This means that many on the team work their own hours, wherever possible, including Maxine's executive assistant, who is always available on her mobile phone. Staff numbers in the office swell during school holidays, as some workers haul their children along too. Team members are also entitled to additional days off – with volunteering for a charity, birthdays, and tenure loyalty reasons for extra days' leave. Assistance is given with out-of-pocket childcare expenses, flowers are sent in the event of a wedding or the birth of a child. 'It's about trying to create that work–family balance,' Maxine says. 'And it is hard in retail as we're a seven-day trading organisation. They don't work seven days, but there are days when they are working weekends, so we try to give a little back. Successful organisations care about their employees and keep them being productive in the business. It isn't about running a commune either. You don't say, "Oh, they have been here 25 years, let's just leave them alone".'

Most of those benefits are driven by Maxine's own parenting experience. 'I sometimes wonder what the culture would be like if I didn't have children,' she says. 'Children mellow you and it's made me appreciate just what women go through. I have been lucky, because I got to design my own little crèche in my office, whereas not every woman gets that opportunity. I had a son that became a 7 am drop-off and a 6 pm pick-up on most days. And does that make me feel guilty? Yes it does! Women can't help but feel guilty. So when anyone comes in here, and says, "My child fell over at school", my instant reaction is, "What are you doing here? Go to them. Because they will always remember you weren't there. I will never remember that you weren't here."'

Mother-guilt drives Maxine to ensure team members have work–life balance. She remembers working through many of her own children's birthdays and school concerts, and perhaps in a bid to make up for that, she still packs lunch for her daughter Grace in high school. 'Someone might look at this building and say it only runs between 9 am and 5 pm. What do I care? Does the job get done? Whether the required job is done in one hour or 25 hours is beside the point, isn't it? Gone are the days where you have to clock in and clock out – you have to trust your people and you can see your team grow every time you give them that trust. For me it's about the law of reciprocation too; if I trust you, you will trust me. If I look after my team, they will look after our customers.'

Of course, equipping team members with the skills and the training to do their job is a significant part of looking after staff. Maxine says some senior people, along the way, have struggled with the idea that they put enormous amounts of time and effort into raising the skill base of those who work at the company – only to see them leave and work for someone else. She has no problem with that; indeed, she's proud of it.

'I get really excited when I see people leave to start their own business or to run their own Telstra licensed store,' she says. 'I think they are going to be successful because we have taught them how to run a business. People don't come into this organisation just to do sales.'

But even that notion took a downward turn during the GFC. The impact of the crisis shook most companies, including Vita Group, from a slumber, and it was in 2009 that the company decided it needed to boost its workers' skills as part of its plan to fight back. Cutting training had left an indelible mark in the minds of many. They considered it an 'easy' cut and Maxine knew they were right; she understood the symbolism attached to it.

'As soon as you cut training, it sends the message that you don't care about people,' Rebecca McLeod says. McLeod was one of those in whom Vita Group invested, having been brought on to develop leadership training. Soon, it developed a life of its own, where team members were trained and acknowledged for their work. Internal benefits included many of those outlined earlier, like extra days off for a birthday, then other benefits were added – like days off to study, an educational allowance, free visits to a counsellor, flu vaccinations, $500 for referring a potential employee that met all probation requirements, and a loyalty purchase program which has been negotiated with several big retailers. Many of these entitlements exist in international firms, but few offer all of them. McLeod says it is paid back over and over again.

'It's proven to drive engagement and retention so we know it's going to pay off in the long run, but it's more than that. It shows that someone is really caring for team members and is willing to put their money where their mouth is.' Evidence proves that the better the employee engagement is, the lower the employee turnover. 'And turnover has a direct link to profitability,' she adds.

Reward and recognition is a sizeable chunk of how an

organisation can look after its team members, especially sales staff who are driven, often by recognition. Vita Group doesn't count the pennies when it hands out rewards, with more than $500,000 each year put aside to take the top team members on an overseas holiday. This commitment is tied to the view, held by Maxine and the leadership team, that the profits of the business can be driven by that middle cohort of workers.

'The purpose of the reward and recognition program is to move the entire bell curve of performance forward,' McLeod says. 'We want to improve everyone, and then we want to differentially reward different groups within the curve depending on what they are doing.'

To that end, the company came up with different rewards programs – one to recognise teams, and another, which has different strands – a shining star program, which every team member can take part in and is best described as a day-to-day, peer-to-peer recognition program, and a pin program where bronze, silver and platinum 'pins' are awarded to sales team members and their managers. McLeod says the shining star program came because they realised there was significant 'top down recognition, but there wasn't a lot of mate-to-mate recognition'.

'So what we do now is send someone a shining star. It's just a way of saying thanks for the hard work you've done. No-one vets it. Everyone looks at what you say because we post them on our intranet – but it doesn't go through an approval process.' Both the shining star and pin programs lead to the Club Success program, where awardees are flown to an overseas location, as a group, for a holiday. Destinations include Los Angeles, Ho Chi Minh City and Hoi An in Vietnam, Oahu and Maui in Hawaii, Phuket in Thailand, Queenstown in New Zealand and New York.

Luke Wadeson started as a part-time salesman at Chermside in Brisbane, working his way up to become an enterprise account executive over the next 14 years. So far, he's travelled to Vietnam, Hawaii, Thailand and Queenstown on the Club Success program.

'The harder you work, the more you are recognised,' he says. He counts the overseas trip as his annual holiday and says it is possible to more than double your salary by working hard. 'My pay packet is a direct reflection of the performance. It's completely measurable. Anyone who is a true salesperson, driven by results, wouldn't stay around unless it was a really rewarding package. I work round the clock but I'm rewarded for it.'

Another reward program, offering profit share, is open to store or business managers and area managers. Targets are set on net profit and recipients pocket a percentage of the amount over that. Both values and customer service are measured and are determined in conversations with line managers. In 2014, one manager earnt an extra $42,000 bonus for a six-month period. The following year, someone received more than $60,000. This is over and above their normal salary, superannuation and monthly commissions.

Training, which was weakened during the global financial crisis, has also been given an expensive reboot. 'We recognise that CARE has multiple facets, including the external customer service component – that is, how do we wow our customer – but it also has a series of internal components focused on how we create a great working environment,' McLeod says. At the heart of the training is an understanding that service is both tangible and intangible, and the intangible part is the most valuable. Customers might not remember exactly how a salesperson went about the sale, but they will remember how they felt. That's the intangible part, and the subject of regular coaching.

Every team member has a tablet with a journal app installed. This becomes their running register of goals, achievements and developments. After new recruit training – which includes face-to-face training and online modules – the tablet serves as a ready-at-hand assistant. Once logged on, a team member can see what they did yesterday and sophisticated software will even recommend what they should focus on today. They have the opportunity to either confirm that or come up with their own focus or goals. The intent is that team members set their own goals with a focus on both the 'what' and the 'how'.

It's been a long journey back after removing those benefits that team members and customers enjoyed before the GFC. It's a trip Maxine does not want to take again.

Left GOLDEN ROMANCE: A young Rose and George Horne, Maxine's grandparents, on a rare holiday in Felixstowe, a seaside town on the North Sea coast of Suffolk.

Right LUNCH DATE: Maxine's father Malcolm takes a break from his gas fitting job. He was in his final year as an apprentice.

Above left BEAR NECESSITY: A seven-year-old Maxine, dressed in her Sunday best, goes on a trip to a Butlin Holiday Park with her cousin Alison, who is two years younger.

Above right HOLIDAY BALL: Maxine being taught volleyball by her grandfather George at a Devon caravan park in 1976. Maxine remembers everyone gathering around the park's single TV to watch David Wilkie win his Olympic gold medal in the 200 m breaststroke.

Below RED ALERT: At the back of her home, each morning, Maxine would change out of her red socks and don the white socks she hid from her parents. The aim was to look like all the other students at St Martin's.

Above RUN HARD: Maxine in a half-marathon in the Rhymney Valley. Running came naturally and offered her a sense of both relaxation and purpose.

Above FIRM FAVOURITES: Maxine's grandparents George and Rose were like parents to Maxine and she made sure, when she started work, that she saw them regularly on weekends. Here, as a 20 year old, she joins them in Suffolk.

Below DRINKS ANYONE: Maxine with her father Malcolm and stepmother Susan, who ran the Railway Hotel in Caerphilly, South Wales. Maxine had come home for the weekend to visit them and their young sons Jason and Anthony.

Top left BOMB DIVE: David takes a jump in the couple's rented Chapel Hill home in 1992. The pool was the home's main drawcard.

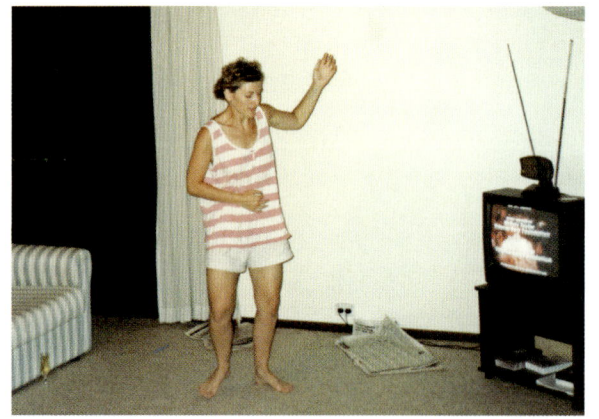

Middle left LADIES' CHOICE: Maxine puts her glass of champagne down at their Chapel Hill home and dances to her own tune. She had just nutted out a strategy that would allow them to go into business on their own.

Bottom left TEAM OPTUS: It was at Optus Communications, where Maxine first worked upon arriving in Australia in 1992, that she met James Bellas. Maxine is in the front row, left. James is behind her to the right.

Above FIT FOR RENOVATION: Maxine and David paid $145,000 in 1993 for their first house in Vaughan Street, Mt Gravatt. The renovation needed to start in the kitchen!

Below FIRST STORE: A phenomenal consumer response followed the opening of the first store at Pacific Fair shopping centre on the Gold Coast. The blue and orange paint was still drying as customers poured through the front door, challenging both stock levels and the couple's growth plans.

Left WORKING MUM: Maxine takes her baby son Jack, who was born in January 1995, to work. He and his younger sister Grace, born in February 1999, were regular office fixtures.

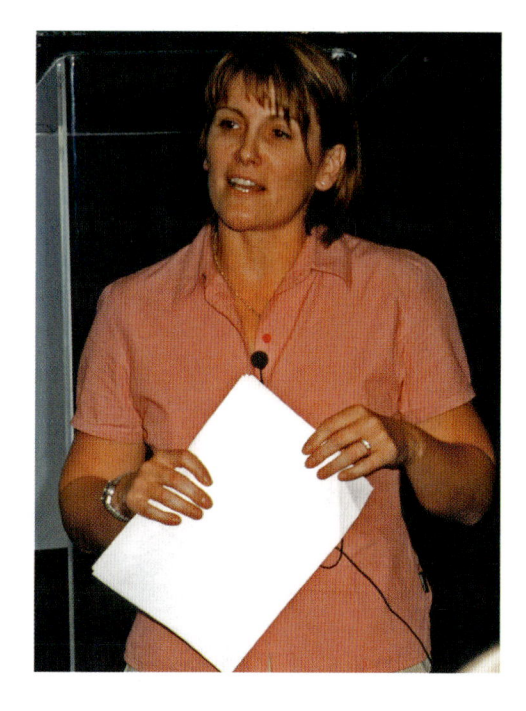

Right ANYONE NEED HELP: Customer service was the hot topic at the 2000 Gold Coast sales conference. Here, Maxine regales her team with stories about how good service can translate to a better bottom line.

Above SUPER POWERS: That was the theme and everyone dressed up at the 2000 Gold Coast sales conference. Maxine, as the tooth fairy, took to the podium under the watchful eye of Wonder Woman – aka her husband David.

Below SMILES ALL ROUND: Club Success in Bali in 2001 where David and Maxine share dinner and a plan to build on their dreams.

Left PHONE RUN: A fun run for thousands, and a terrific marketing opportunity for Fone Zone – so David donned an orange skin suit and headed out in runners.

Below MILLIONAIRES' ROW: All the blood, sweat and tears paid off and Maxine and David built a stunning, multi-million-dollar family home – a stark contrast to their first house. After a protracted property settlement, David and his former Personal Assistant (now his second wife) moved into the home, which has since been sold.

In Maxine's Words

'If we came into another GFC, I would make sure that we did not pull those benefits. I would look at what else we can pull. Let's go back and negotiate hard on suppliers. Let's go out to the sales team. One of the things I wish I had done and I didn't do was to go out and say, "Guys, we are in the middle of a financial crisis here and these are my options – I can pull CARE. I can make X amount of people redundant. Or we can all take a 10 per cent salary cut. You tell me what you want me to do." I really wish I had done that because I honestly believe that they would have come back and said we will take a cut.'

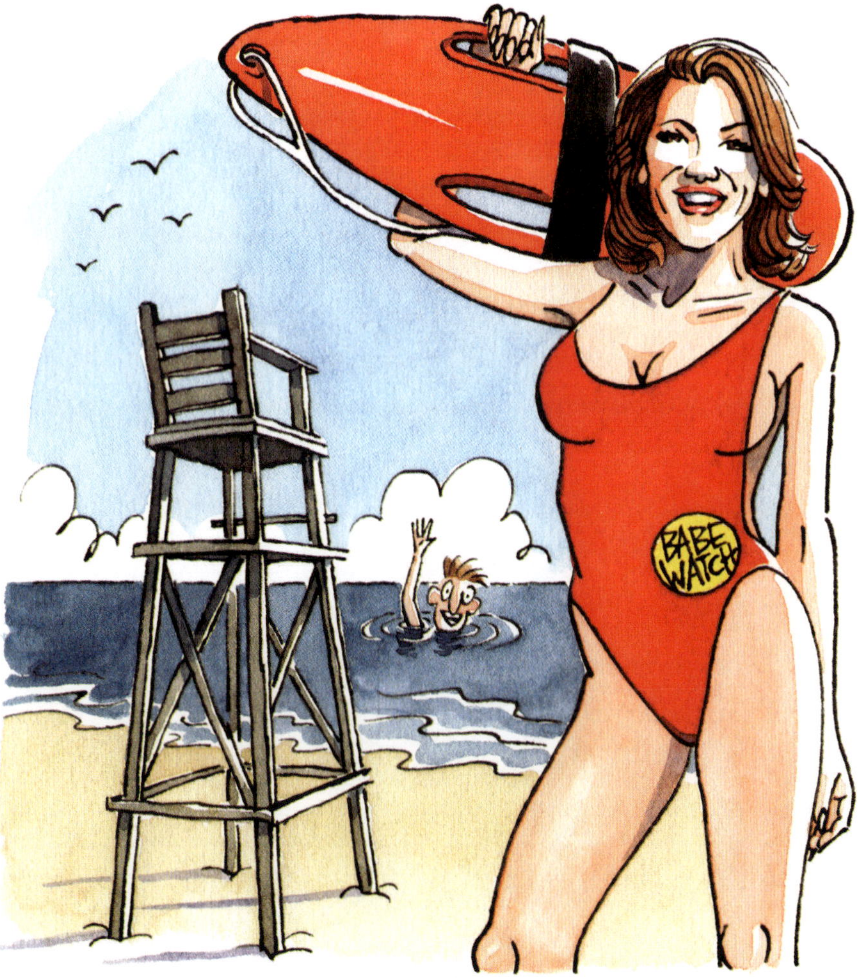
BABE WATCH

7.

Lead, Don't Just Manage

'Before you are a leader, success is all about growing yourself. When you become a leader, success is all about growing others.' – Jack Welch, former CEO of General Electric

When Maxine talks about leadership, she goes to the beach. 'The analogy I use is surf lifesaving,' she says. 'You've got the lifesaver walking up and down the beach, close to the water, and what he's looking for are the little toddlers, any immediate threat posed by the shallow waters, and whether any of those little ones are separated from their carers. That's one level of protection. Then you have the lifesaver who is out on the waves on a jet ski. His view is broader: making sure no-one is in danger swimming. And then you have another layer of protection: the person up in the clubhouse who's looking further out to make sure that there's not a shark loitering, or a huge swell developing. That is your leadership team. It's the same with my business. The leader is in the clubhouse, looking at the entire picture. That's how I like to run it.'

The analogy highlights the difference between management and leadership. Maxine's team members are the swimmers, with middle and senior management taking on the role of lifesavers. Her leadership team, including her chief operating officer and chief financial officer, is sitting up in the chief lifesaver's chair, watching over proceedings, with a strategy to act quickly and skilfully when needed. They are eyeing it all, from slightly further away. The shark might amount to an issue on the risk register, or a big swell might hint at a looming economic issue.

'Up in the clubhouse, the leader needs to survey the whole scene – with an eye on the upcoming weather, funding decisions, and how the public is using the beach. I find people like to mystify business and make it more difficult than it is,' Maxine says.

That doesn't mean the road to leadership is easy. First you need to understand your team, or the swimmers in your story. Next you need to understand the role and the reach of each of your lifesavers, or middle managers on the floor, and finally – and often this is the biggest step

– you need to leave the beach for the clubhouse and let those you employ in your senior management team act.

Leaders also need to allow their team to make mistakes. Hundreds of books have been written about leadership, but strip them down and a few character traits come up repeatedly. Leaders need to be authentic. They need to set an example by practising what they preach. And they need to flourish in bad times, as well as good.

'There are so many good-time leaders and I mean that in a derogatory way,' Maxine says. 'When times are great, anyone can be a leader. It's what happens during the downturns that matter. And leaders have to be able to accept change and act on it quickly.' There are generic traits that run across industries, and the technological and online revolution we've seen in the past decade has stopped many would-be leaders in their tracks. It wasn't the change; it was the inability to adapt to the change. There's a litany of casualties in business and industry – Kodak, Blockbuster, Borders, most of the newspaper industry – all victims of acting too late or believing they could somehow avoid the forces sweeping around them.

Maxine believes a good leader needs to take regular advice, which is why she agreed to her chair Dick Simpson's suggestion that she visit an executive coach. On Simpson's recommendation, she put in a call to Rupert Bryce. It's helping her leapfrog the different mindsets – from salesperson and company owner, along the management trajectory – to leadership. It's an ongoing journey, and will remain so until she hangs up her high

Lessons in business leadership from **Maxine Horne**

heels (or 'killer wheels' as she likes to call them).

It's a common view in Australian boardrooms and offices of executive coaches that a company owner will not innately show all the gifts of a good leader. That's primarily because they have invested so much of their personal time and energy in the success of the business – the 'third child' syndrome discussed earlier. They will not have done a 360-degree assessment, or completed any workplace psychology testing. More often than not they will have a 'if it's not being done properly I'll just do it myself' mentality. Similarly, a person who is considered a talented manager will not always grow into a respected leader – just as it is possible too to have a visionary leader who would not win any accolades as the company's best manager. That's where executive coaches and the cut-and-thrust of board discussions can help those on the journey to leadership.

Dick Simpson believes leaders are not always born but their skills can be learnt. Rupert Bryce, who acts as an executive coach to dozens of leaders including Maxine, says a leader's role constantly evolves. 'It's about how the leader reads and understands each person and gets them aligned and focused.' On that basis, a CEO is about one-quarter manager and three-quarters leader.

Maxine's lessons in business leadership spill from each chapter of this book. Under each of them, she has a series of personal steps that she works on. In the staircase to leadership, she's imported 11 points that act as her personal creed.

1. Know yourself and seek self-improvement

This aligns with Maxine's determination to seek advice, mull it over, and decide whether to act on it. But to do that, she's had to learn to be brutally honest with herself. What are your strengths and weaknesses? What do you need to address? Maxine suggests self-study, formal classes, reflection, or an executive coach. A good relationship with members of your board or executive helps here too. 'You have to have an honest understanding of who you are, what you know, what you can do and of course what you can't do,' she says. She gives the example of a rich part of town – whether it's Brisbane or Sydney or Melbourne – where people talk about themselves constantly, their successes and their wealth. 'The reality is that they are all fur coat and no knickers. I've learnt over time that people who talk about it in spades actually don't have it – whether it be money, or a relationship, or integrity.' The second point is you need to be aware that it is your team – not you – who determines whether you are successful. If your team does not trust you, or lacks confidence in you, then they will be uninspired and unlikely to follow you. To be successful, you have to convince your team, not yourself or your board, that you are worthy of being followed.

2. Be technically proficient and set the example

As a leader, you must know your job inside-out and be familiar with what your team does. That doesn't mean you need to perform those tasks yourself, but that you know how they are done. 'How else do you decipher the bullshit from the truth? In my opinion, if you expect somebody else to do something, then you should be able to do it yourself.' To that end, Maxine has, over time, worked in every part of the company. She doesn't turn it into a royal visit, but over the years has regularly turned up at morning meetings. Along the way, she's also grabbed a duster, welcomed customers, and sold them phones. 'You need to be a good role model for your team. It is not good enough for them to hear from you what they are expected to do – they must also see it from you.'

3. Seek responsibility and take responsibility for your actions

Don't hide from challenges, or the decisions made. 'Search for ways to guide your organisation to new heights,' Maxine says. 'And when things go wrong, as they always do sooner or later, try not to blame others.' Maxine has made numerous mistakes, and many are the subject of the lessons in this book. But, with each one of them, she's found the opportunity to learn. 'Want to do better? Learn new things.'

4. Make sound and timely decisions

It's critical to use good problem-solving, decision-making and planning tools when you make decisions. 'But not making a decision is worse than making a wrong one,' Maxine says. Similarly, Maxine tells her team that executing an okay strategy will always win out over not executing a brilliant one. 'You need to be able to show leadership courage as well. And if the decision you make is wrong, you need to be flexible enough to change course or tweak the path ahead. Pride can wait for another day.'

5. Know your people and look out for their wellbeing

Different people require different styles of leadership. 'For example, someone new to Vita Group requires more supervision than an experienced team member,' Maxine says. 'A team member who lacks motivation requires a different approach than one with a high degree of motivation.' Every situation is different too, and what you do in one might not work in another. 'You may need to confront an employee for inappropriate behaviour, but if the confrontation is too late or too early, too harsh or too weak, then the results may prove ineffective.' It's not important to be the office agony aunt; having your team's wellbeing at heart is where it's at. 'One of the guys here – his house got flooded. He had just had a little baby, so we all pitched in, with 20 of us going to his house and cleaning. Then we established a fund where all Vita Group team members could donate and the company would match their donations. At the end of that, the company chipped in an extra $20,000 (which was divided between four recipients). For me, that's about looking after them.' She says this has an added advantage. 'When someone gets headhunted, it's now not ever about the money. A whole lot of things come into play, including the emotional engagement they have with us.'

6. Keep your team involved. Communicate. Communicate. Communicate.

'I have often heard people say, "Oh, we can't tell them this", and I go, "Why?" You've got to trust your people,' Maxine says. 'Yes, it might get out, but in the whole scheme of things, how big is that?' She says a mistake that business leaders often made is that they use knowledge as power negatively. 'They keep it all to themselves because they think I am the leader and I am the only person who should know this – when if they actually passed that knowledge on, they'd have a lot more power.' Vita Group's retail store managers are called business managers and are encouraged to run their local stores as a small business, winning a profit share as part of a reward and recognition system. 'Some people said to me, "What if they leave and set up their own Telstra store?" I say that they will and I would be exceptionally proud of that because it shows how much good work they did on the way to getting there.' Once you've learnt how to communicate, you should then 'over-communicate!'.

7. Develop a sense of responsibility in your team

Maxine has found this lesson the hardest, and on some days she still fights the urge to do more than she should; to climb back up that lifesaver's chair rather than stay in the clubhouse. 'You have to take responsibility for the team but that doesn't mean that you can't have a team that's not responsible,' she says. Maxine says it's only in the last five years that she's learnt the value of climbing off the jet ski and letting others take it out. 'You have to understand that as the business grows, your team either grows with it or they stay in the roles they are in. That was an emotional lesson for me to learn, but also I didn't quite get what my board was telling me.' Maxine could only see the job in front of her, and wanted to get it done. 'Being able to step back is a real skill of a leader. There is a lot of trust involved, and a fair amount of self-discipline needed.' Mistakes will be made. But the bottom line is you must encourage good business traits in your team that will help them to carry out their professional responsibilities and develop their long-term careers.

8. Ensure that the tasks are understood, supervised and accomplished

When you communicate something, make sure you are addressing the target audience. 'It's no good me going into a store and talking high-level strategy – because it's the wrong group to address. It should be about "what I need you to do, how I need you to do it, why I need you to do it, and when I need you to do it by". Then take a step back,' she says. Maxine has a phrase for this: inspect what you expect. Metrics matter and are used daily and voluminously to do exactly that. 'So as much as it is great to stand back and let things happen, you have to make sure that they are actually happening.'

9. Train as a team

Too many leaders call their organisation, department or unit a 'team' when it's not. 'They are just a group of people doing their individual jobs,' Maxine says. 'But you'll always get more out of a group of people than you will out of an individual.' The ability to be competitive, but to work as an integral part of a functioning team, is always the subject of investigation at recruitment level. 'If you are training as a team you are encouraging each other, you are seeing different perspectives, prompting diversity in the decision making,' she says. She reminds her team that although she has felt the rush of going it alone, the better result has always stemmed from a considered team strategy.

10. Use the full capabilities of your company

Team spirit will drive greater success, Maxine says, and there is virtue in genuinely using the skills and talents of those you employ. Remember, always, to credit their ideas. It means, next time, there will be no cap on the ideas meetings.

11. Never ever assume that you know it all

Each day you need to reflect on your own behaviour and ask yourself this question: could I have done better? 'I've learnt that I can always get better and I can always learn from those around me,' Maxine says.

•

Maxine warns emerging leaders of a phenomenon called 'the shadow of a leader'. She used to flare up and move on five minutes later, forgetting the issue that momentarily inflamed her. What she didn't realise was that the episode could linger. The Post-it note story mentioned earlier in this book involved Maxine banning Post-it notes in an early moment of authoritarianism. A year or two later, a new employee asked gingerly whether he could order some Post-it notes. 'What do you mean?' Maxine replied, forgetting she had once banned them. 'I was oblivious to the fact that, ever since I had done that, there was an embargo on Post-it notes!'

It's not just a fit of fury that can follow a leader. A quirky sense of humour that others don't find funny is another case in point. 'As a leader you are never off-duty. People look at how you dress, how you behave, what you say and the tone in which you say it. You set the tone. You cast a long shadow and it's either positive or negative. If there is something wrong with your team the first place you need to look is yourself. People will duplicate what they see. They will emulate you.'

Leaders need to foster an environment in which others can flourish. 'If your team isn't growing then your business isn't growing,' Maxine says. 'Often I see leaders who are jealous of the people who work for them and take credit for what they've done. That is a big, big no-no. People won't want to work for you. People want to work for recognition, and one of the recognition points is people knowing that they have achieved something.' If it's done right, Maxine says, leaders will also take pride in seeing members of their team move on to bigger and better careers. 'Leaders are really mentors — or should become strong mentors,' she says. Maxine has used two career mentors (an early manager and her board chair), and an executive coach, and attributes their advice to her ability to look at the company's strategy from the clubhouse, not from the water.

That first mentor, Tricia Mittens, coached Maxine in sales as she teetered on the list of those the company might 'let go'. Mittens says she found Maxine was a sponge for knowledge. 'The reason it wasn't working before was because no-one was giving her the direction she needed.' That's a salient point. Sometimes, the fault of a non-performing team member can be attributed to the leader, and whether they are skilled at seeing — and addressing — those deficiencies. 'I really wonder if Tricia hadn't have been there, what I'd be doing?' Maxine says. 'And that's had a huge influence on how I run this business. I talk about the power of a leader; you have no idea the value that you can add, not just to someone at work, but to their whole life.'

Rarely are those leadership traits evident at an early age, and Maxine tells two stories of her early management experience that fly in the face of the leadership rungs she's been able to climb ever since. The first was in Birmingham, England, where she was in charge of a small satellite office for Mercury Paging. The office was above a kebab shop.

'It was disgusting,' Maxine says. 'We tolerated the smell but over a period of time I got chatting to some of the other offices [of the same company]. They had these plush offices – so I negotiated for us to move in with them.' But – and it's a big but – she didn't tell anyone, least of all her superiors. She didn't think she needed to: it was vacant space and didn't cost any extra money. To Maxine, it was a win-win situation: better digs, at no cost, without the constant smell of kebabs. It worked until about four weeks later, when her managers found out she was no longer at the assigned company office. Neither were her co-workers. The lesson: there is a good pathway to doing things and seeking authorisation is a sound place to start.

The second example occurred while Maxine was in the same position. One of her salesmen was tardy, regularly turning up late for meetings without thinking that behaviour was unacceptable. Talking to him didn't work.

'I used to have conversation after conversation with him and would say, "I don't know what is so hard about being on time". I was given excuse after excuse and I didn't want to hear it anymore, so I told him that if he was a minute late, in future, I would simply lock him out of the room. Full stop.' True to her word, the following week, with the morning meeting in progress, there was a knock on the door. Maxine knew it was her salesman, with his usual late entry. But instead of opening the door, Maxine put into practice her promise.

'I went over and he thinks I'm going to open the door – and I pull the blind down.' Their working relationship did not improve, and while these are small examples, they illustrate the point that it's hard to lead before you learn to lead, and leadership by nature means taking your employees with you on the journey to success. Locking a key salesman out of meetings was not a proven pathway to a bigger profit.

Maxine's journey to leadership has been accelerated by her board chair and main mentor Dick Simpson, whose first request was for her to visit an executive coach. Simpson says those who don't make the leap from manager to CEO are unable to adapt to a significantly different role. Over time, it was Simpson who also encouraged Maxine to take a step back, to see the board as a help rather than a hindrance, and to learn that a good negotiation ends with both sides believing they have won something.

Simpson talks about a capability study he once

read which showed that leaders go through a series of 'capability levels'. Very few people reach that final top level, where visionaries like Nelson Mandela might sit, but those on the way move through the levels in a bid to reach a proficiency, feel comfortable in it, before moving on. 'At a low level you might have a plumber who wants to own his own business and not worry about anything else. He's got a capability level and no interest in changing that,' Simpson says. As you climb the levels, strategy and how to execute it becomes more crucial. And he says Maxine continues to ascend. The end point is that clubhouse, or the leader's chair, where both the threats and opportunities can be assessed close-up and at a distance simultaneously.

In Maxine's Words

In trying to be a good leader, I focus on three things:
1. What I am – and that includes my values, beliefs and character.
2. What I know – such as jobs, tasks and human nature. And it's important here to also remember what I don't know.
3. What I do – such as implementing, motivating and providing direction.

Coaching a Leader: Six Skills for Leaders by executive coach Rupert Bryce

1. Put it in perspective
The first thing a coach can do for a leader is to help them gain perspective on what they are looking at, how they are looking at it, and also help them gain a better understanding of their own thinking processes. Often, the challenge is to overcome a common thinking bias or trap of looking in one particular direction. For some leaders, this might be focusing too much on the past, for others it might be spending too much time thinking of goals in the distant future. The goal of coaching is to assist leaders in taking new directions and perspectives that enrich their thinking and remove them from those pitfalls and biases.

2. Clarify a purpose and get aligned
In complex work environments and larger businesses, it is easy to lose sight of the bigger picture and what you are there to achieve. By providing direction, not directing, leaders are able to better understand their role, what the purpose of the organisation is and what everyone can do to fulfil that purpose.

3. Strengthen and connect your team
Unified around a cohesive, connected purpose, a leader's job is to facilitate the building of trust, ownership and accountability within the team. The most high-functioning teams are the ones that consist of individuals who take responsibility for their purpose and feel and act more accountable to their peers.

4. Be a leader of change
Connected to the evolving purpose of the organisation, leaders should strive to be innovators for change by providing a compelling view of the future. By offering something worthwhile on the horizon for both employees and the organisation, leaders are able to assist in keeping individuals motivated through the change process and aligned towards reaching common goals.

5. Build capability

One of the most crucial roles of a leader is to develop people through both supporting and challenging them to be their best. When leaders create an accurate self-awareness of performance levels and development areas in their staff, far less time is required for managing performance issues in the future. This investment in building capability is not always easy or obvious with the challenges of running a business.

6. Manage emotions

Emotions are powerful drivers of performance at work and knowing how to harness and leverage them is a critical leadership skill. By firstly managing their own emotions, leaders are better equipped to guide their employees' emotions in positive ways to drive performance.

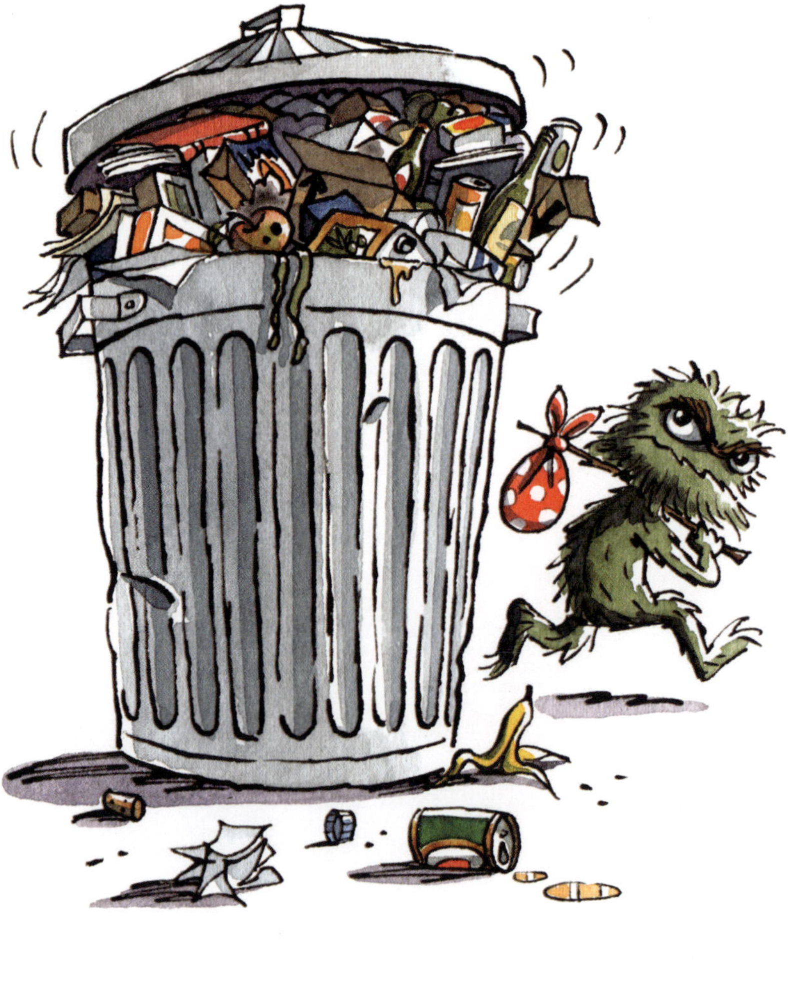

8.

Take Your Partners

'It is rare to find a business partner who is selfless. If you are lucky, it happens once in a lifetime.' – Michael Eisner, former CEO of the Walt Disney Company

When you pick a partner in life, the character traits that appeal to you shine brightly. Perhaps you even tick off those variables or personality quirks that are important to you. More common than not, a similar set of goals or values will rate highly. You need to respect what each of you brings to the relationship. Communication is crucial, especially as the partnership stretches across years, and the need to be able to articulate differences and solve problems by talking, and listening, has been found, time and time again, to assist. Initially, during the heady times of a new romance, it might be the differences you treasure. Negotiation will come easy; overlooking the bathroom towel on the floor, clothes piled in a hallway, not putting the bins out, or even the coffee cup that ends each night beside the television remote in the lounge room. With time, you might become proficient at biting your tongue too, for the sake of long-term harmony, or even for the household economics. Your focus will be on what can be achieved, not torn down, and you'll always consider the bigger picture. Relationships flourish when both people remain committed and working towards a common goal.

Developing a business partnership is no different. A corporate courtship involves finding a business with similar values and synergies; some other organisation that sees benefit in travelling along the same path. Both partners need to bring something to the table so that the sum of what they offer advantages their individual brands. Negotiation needs to lead the parties to the 'sweet spot', where both are able to commit to a deal where they trust each other. And often that means compromise too; leaving behind a loved part of the brand or strategy that worked yesterday, but might not necessarily tomorrow.

Fone Zone had formed a close partnership with Telstra in 1995 with a Telstra dealer agreement, which was renewed repeatedly, before the exclusive licence was signed in 2009. That latter agreement allowed Vita

Group to transform its Fone Zone network into Telstra retail outlets, enjoying the brand recognition that comes with the Telstra colours and logo. The partners did not always agree, but it was clear to everyone sitting around the negotiating table that both Telstra and Fone Zone were reaping rewards from the partnership.

In 2012, however, Vita Group did a deal that was not in the interests of both parties and no amount of hindsight can change this fact. Maxine acknowledges this, but she learnt some valuable lessons along the way, not least the importance of respect. It also highlights other attributes she's grown to value in the CEO's office: a determination to speak up if a decision made by others sits uncomfortably; a willingness to admit a mistake made by her company and to take responsibility for it; and a resolve to ask question, after question, until every one of them is answered. It's advice she passes on generously to others. 'We stuffed up,' she admits. 'We realised that, and it would never happen again.'

In a nutshell, Vita Group entered into a licence agreement to sell a waterproofing protection called Liquipel to mobile customers. 'Liquipel protects against accidental water contact by penetrating the entire mobile device, including all of the vital internal components,' Vita Group announced at the time. 'This cutting edge technology deposits a coating 1000 times thinner than a human hair to all parts of the device, both internally and externally. Invisible to the naked eye, it won't compromise the look, feel, or performance.' That was all well and good, but in this case, only one partner was interested in the new technology. Telstra was not.

Vita Group went ahead anyway and offered Liquipel in all its stores, including those branded as Telstra. This was at a time when mobile phone consumption was fanning out across all demographics, and indeed, in April 2012, the Australian Bureau of Statistics recorded 818,500 children aged five to 14 years had a mobile phone – almost 30 per cent. About 82 million of the world's mobile phones were water damaged each year. And that provided a new market for Vita Group to use Liquipel which worked along these lines: phones could be sprayed in a special oven with a fine coating that would then prevent any water from seeping in. In simple terms, it made the phone waterproof, and that appealed to consumers who wanted to protect their own mobile or that of their child. To some inside the Vita Group, it seemed like a no-brainer; an accessory that would have customers lining up to buy, and one that provided customers with additional value.

Telstra, however, did not share that enthusiasm. It was more cautious, wanting more time to conduct tests on the product to ensure that it was right for the Telstra brand. Timing is crucial in business; any small delay can be the difference between being first and last, and the Vita Group struggled to countenance a time delay. Gut decisions are important too, and Vita Group had a history of being courageous – and right. Its decision to put mobile phone stores into shopping centres was seen as foolhardy by many, but the queues of customers soon proved the doubters wrong. Maxine and David were entrepreneurial and savvy and knew risk always played a part in any business decision.

Telstra has always been more cautious, and rightly so; building a strong brand based on a measured and strategic approach to new initiatives and its risk appetite was fed on a more prudent approach. But Vita Group pressed on, knowing that there was only a short window of it becoming commercially viable. (Indeed, that latter point proved right; manufacturers down the track moved to use something similar in the mobile phone manufacturing process, not as a separate product.) Maxine was in hospital having back surgery when the Liquipel decision was made, and there is no doubt if she could go back in time, she would have put a lot of questions to those leading the Liquipel charge. 'A CEO – even a joint one – doesn't make excuses, though,' she says now.

The decision by Vita Group to enter into an agreement with Liquipel equated to one partner suggesting a Christmas holiday to Canada without any real analysis of how it might affect the household or budget plans, or even whether the other partner had any annual leave accrued. And then when the partner objects or wants to check the finances – or even expresses a desire to stay home to celebrate – the other takes off on the plane. The discussion that follows is always going to be fraught. The mistake, here, was Vita Group proceeding without its partner's support. 'I think people learnt a valuable lesson,' Maxine says now. 'You wouldn't go ahead like that if you really respected the relationship and I've made sure everyone here knows that.'

Vita Group was the custodian of the Telstra brand in the marketplace. And the decision to move forward, without its partner's support, flew in the face of the historic agreement the two businesses had forged in 2009.

Tony Pearson, who worked for Telstra at the time of the Liquipel deal (before later joining Vita Group), remembers Telstra's response. 'It was not approved and you can't do it – that was Telstra's clear response,' Pearson says.

Telstra then stepped in and determined that Liquipel could not be sold in those stores that had been branded as Telstra. This meant it was only available through Fone Zone stores. That immediately cooled its potential, and eventually Maxine shut it down. 'To her credit I have seen her actually apologise to Telstra and senior managers saying that Vita Group didn't handle it correctly and that we have learnt from it,' Pearson says. But not before a cost to Vita Group of more than $700,000, and a bit of varnish being rubbed off its relationship with Telstra.

The Liquipel story provides a valuable lesson in building effective relationships. And that's because it had the potential to strongly damage the partnership. 'We had to open the kimono about the things we had done wrong,' one senior employee says. That meant admitting to its partner that the decision had been a mistake. Vita Group took a step back and re-evaluated what it meant to Telstra – and what Telstra meant to it.

'It was a turning point,' Maxine says now. And it required a real shift in how Vita Group saw its partnership; a shift that feeds its robust relationship today. Vita Group became more conciliatory. It listened more. The leadership team worked assiduously to assure Telstra that the two parties were once more aligned. The bottom line, as Maxine points out, is that it should never have come to that. The Liquipel agreement should never have happened. Telstra and Vita Group had enjoyed a strong partnership, going back 17 years at the time, and pursuing a plan like this, without respecting the view of the other partner, was always going to present difficulties. In the end, Telstra lost nothing. Vita Group lost money and face.

•

Maxine Horne has always been a fighter. As a child, she fought to find out where she belonged. As a teenager, she accepted every challenge that came her way with a determination to come first, never second. As a young worker, she demanded all staff – male and female, young and old – take their turn in making coffee and she was happy to stare down her superiors to make it happen. She loved to win, but she also gave the impression she liked the scrap too. Blessed with street smarts not taught at university and a work ethic that intimidated others, she didn't like giving ground as far as her business was concerned. She knew, in theory, that she had to eventually temper that. Even her chairman Dick Simpson – her 'wise old owl' in her words – had counselled her along those lines.

Those who have started and run their own successful small businesses will know the spot in which Maxine found herself. The early mornings at work, the evenings that crept past midnight while still working on the dining room table, the anxiety that wakes you from a slumber, over something small, but important.

'It was my third child,' Maxine says. And that makes it hard to let others in; to let partners have an equal say in the path ahead. 'But it is so important to do that. The relationship you forge is bigger than any one business decision – and that realisation was behind our decision to quickly exit the Liquipel product.'

This brings us squarely to a discussion on building a successful negotiation – whether it's in the initial partnership talks, or discussing a joint venture down the track. Greg Robertson, who led the private equity investment in Fone Zone by Investec Wealth and who served as a non-executive director, puts it this way: 'Sometimes you've got to take a step backwards or sideways to lose a skirmish but win the war. And it's rare in life to get the perfect outcome, so you've got to settle for the best you can do in the circumstances at the time.' Robertson points to a comment Maxine made back in

2005 that shows she has always understood the value of a partner. 'On the day that we listed on the ASX, a journalist said to Maxine, "Don't you feel like an idiot. You've just listed this business – it's worth $150 million – you sold a third of it for $8 million a couple of years ago. Didn't Investec buy into it too cheaply?"'

Maxine's reaction was genuine and speedy. 'Not at all,' she replied. 'We would never have got there without a partner.'

Banks are another crucial partner and Maxine's experience there has modified her behaviour too. In the early days, she was suspicious and adversarial. 'We saw them as people who said "no", but over the years I've learnt that you get more from people if you treat them with respect,' she says. 'Banks get really nervous if they don't know stuff. If you are going to partner with someone you really have to share all the information and take them on the journey that you are taking everyone else on as well.' While Vita Group's status as a publicly listed company provides its banks with all the information it wants, every six months Maxine sits down with her bankers to explain the company's strategy and where it is headed. 'That would be my advice to anyone starting in small business. View your banker as your partner and treat them as such. Make sure they understand your strategy. And even if you have bad news, tell them – and tell them how you are dealing with it and how you are addressing it. Don't try and hide it from them and don't sweep it under the carpet and hope it goes away. It won't.'

Maxine says negotiation is an art that requires practice, respect and maintenance. 'First, you need to know your "drop dead" position. What will you give away and at what point do you say, "I'm done"?' That point is akin to a weekend house auction, where a purchaser sets a cap and will withdraw if bidding slides past it. 'Second, you need to ensure some flexibility in your position. Third, you have to make sure you leave those negotiations with each other's respect and the ability to continue working together.'

Maxine still plays to win, but there are other paths to victory than a slam-dunk early in the match. 'You can go in damn hard – like I used to – but you will have to come back to the table. Over time, I've learnt the hard way that you are always likely to attract more bees with honey.' It's a lesson she's learnt again recently, in her divorce settlement. 'You have to think of the big picture and work out the small battles you are prepared to lose.'

In Maxine's Words

Q. How did you go into negotiations early on in your career?

A: I had just one thought: I wanted to win everything and I wanted no survivors and if you were down I was going to make sure you never got back up again. I even accused someone senior at Telstra of lying. I swore at him, and all the men in the room were thinking, 'Who is this woman?'. (Maxine believed the executive had lied to her over a tangential issue.) I would not speak to him for about 18 months after that. Now I think how rude I must have sounded. I know I used to piss off a lot of people. I have a natural blunt temperament. That said, we're now good friends.

Q. Who called you out on it?

A. My chair eventually said to me, 'A good negotiation is when both parties feel they have given something away.'

Q. When did he say that to you?

A. When I was negotiating my divorce settlement. Now in business, I've learnt that it's just about being realistic, and being able to compromise.

Q. So how have you changed as a negotiator?

A. Now my team does it. Of course I'm there, and I'll sit quietly which sometimes freaks the other side out, especially if they knew me from times gone by. I know I can have my say at any time and often those on the other side will say, 'What do you think, Maxine?' but I've learnt that negotiation can be done in several ways. For me, now, keeping calm, thinking about the big picture and curtailing my natural inclination to fight works for me … plus I also have a team of great negotiators around me.

Q. What if you were giving advice to someone younger who is just starting to negotiate?

A. Play the ball not the man. And be respectful, because people are just doing their jobs. Their job is to do the best thing for their company and your job is to do the best thing for yours. You forget, when you are younger, that there often is a war to win as well as a few battles along the way. Don't burn your bridges because, trust me, you will need to go back over them and I think that is relevant whether it is in your business or in your personal life.

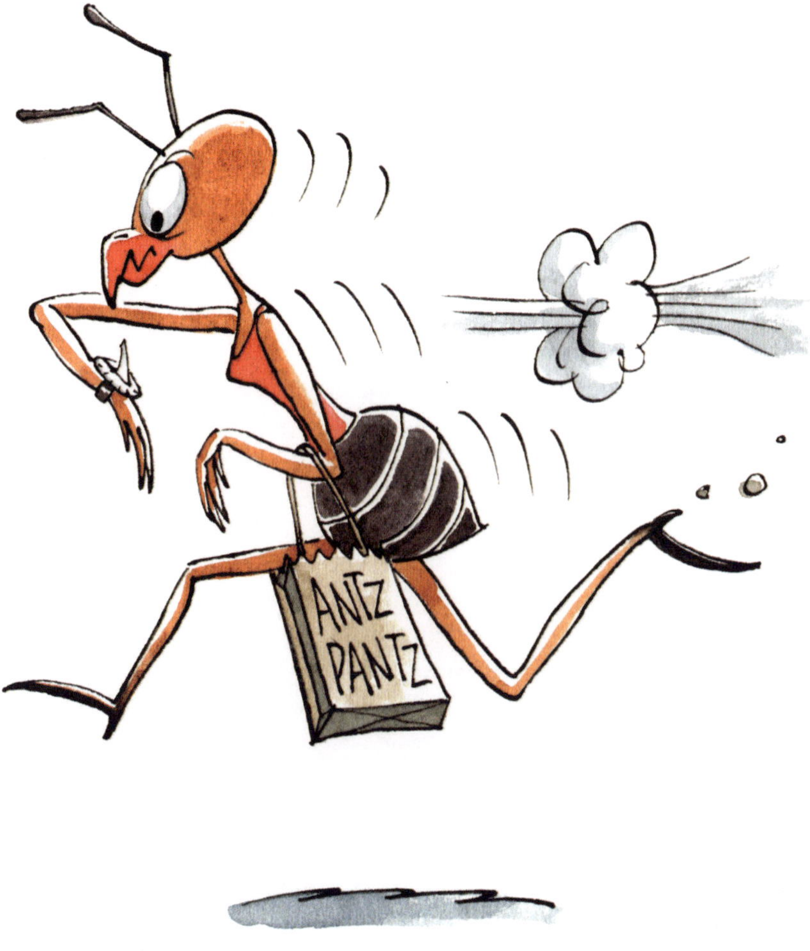

ANTZ
PANTZ

9.

Follow the Ant Trail

'The ants go marching one by one. Hurrah. Hurrah.' – Robert D. Singleton, nursery rhyme writer

Ants rely on a scent trail, left by their scouts, to guide their colonies. The smell, which registers through the ants' antennae, steers the troops towards food. Maxine believes people's shopping habits are similar, and learning to follow the customer 'ant trail' is a simple skill that is lost on many small businesses who lease space to sell their goods.

At most shopping centres, customers prefer to park close to a centre entrance: it saves time, makes it easier for them to carry their purchases, and even wrangle children in and out of baby seats. That's the first thing to note, Maxine says. But then almost invariably the customer is going to use the closest point of entry to the shopping centre. That's when the ant trail Maxine follows comes in. As customers surge through the limited number of entrances, they follow a path. They walk with purpose, intent on getting what they need. At this stage, they are focused on picking up the purchase and leaving via the same door they entered. But after a matter of minutes, or tens of metres, they hit what Maxine terms a 'wander zone', where they are more prepared to wander than walk, to contemplate everything from a coffee to a robot vacuum cleaner. That's when they're prepared to be entertained. And that's the best spot, according to Maxine, to set up commercial camp.

'Food courts help too because people will sit and look around as they eat. Many of them will finish and think, "I'll just nip in over there". That's how sales happen.'

It's a philosophy Maxine learnt early on from a project manager, and a lesson that has made the cash register ring over and over again.

'The first thing I look at is where the busiest car park in any shopping centre is, because that's where people will park and that's their planned entry,' she says. 'But I try to avoid the first 20 metres from the moment they enter the centre.' That's because the customer's 'intent' has kicked in, and their mind is racing with the jobs they have to do. 'Watch the stores in those first 20 metres. I never see them very busy and that's why.'

In an age where anything and everything can be purchased online, retailers need to focus on providing relaxation and even diversion to entice customers away from the drudgery of their planned excursion.

'Shopping today is about entertainment as much as making a purchase and the proof of that is you can get anything now online,' Maxine says. 'The "wander zone" is where people are wandering around having a look, open to buying something they didn't specifically arrive to buy. And you have to be in that sweet spot in any shopping centre for them to walk through your front door.' None of this is news to centre lease managers and it's no accident that rents are higher in the wander zones.

Fone Zone was early to embrace the idea of the ant trail, but along the way a communications colony developed. 'We knew we were really onto something so we took the business plan and rapidly rolled it out as we could afford,' Maxine says. 'But what we found was that some landlords, bless them, were approaching other telco retailers and requesting they open because we were really doing well.' Before long, there was fierce competition for sites – both in terms of location and price. That led to centres developing small 'cluster industries', which is why you now often find all the telco providers in the same area of a big shopping centre. That consolidation has forced providers to offer a point of difference, and that's why consumer behaviour has also increased the focus on customer service. According to Maxine, the ants will behave in one way, but you can influence the trail by providing the best source of food.

Maxine says the clustering of telcos forced Fone Zone to re-examine consumer behaviours and how it might provide 'additional scents to the ant trail' to force consumers to stop at their store, not the ones on either side. 'And it reinforced my view that customers will pay more if the service provided is above and beyond a purchase,' she says.

Dr Violet Lazarevic from the Australian Centre for Retail Studies at Monash Business School has not heard of Maxine's 'ant trail' expression, but she says it mirrors strongly consumer behaviour. Dr Lazarevic says consumers typically have two reasons to visit a shopping centre – a hedonic need or a utilitarian need.

'If they are utilitarian-focused it means they'll have a goal in mind,' she says. 'These types of consumers will go in and head for whatever they came in for and not deviate too much. They might stop and have some food and then be attracted to some stores around the food court if they have the time to do that.' These consumers are less likely to want to make a discretionary purchase but are increasingly becoming more important to telcos like the Vita Group because mobile phones are increasingly being seen as a necessary item.

Dr Lazarevic says those consumers after a 'hedonic experience' are a very different type of consumer. 'That's somebody who comes in for the pleasure of shopping.' And they sit squarely in Maxine's target zone too.

The science of consumer behaviour is used widely by business owners who will try to snag a space near a big department store (sometimes referred to as a 'destination store'), because it will be located along a busy thoroughfare. Likewise, once inside a store, the science of consumer spending continues. For example, there's a reason why cosmetics, not fridges, are placed at the entrance of big department stores.

'You want whatever is appealing to be at the front of the department store,' Dr Lazarevic says. 'That's why you'll often see discounted items or very visually appealing items. If someone is going on a hedonic shopping trip they are looking for colour and for visual attraction, and variety.'

It's a science Maxine has understood intuitively from day one. But she has made mistakes along the way. 'The whole reason we went into kiosks was because we saw the monthly rent was lower – but nine times out of 10 there is a reason why it's lower,' she says. Fone Zone jumped into kiosks early – and left them quickly. Team members hated working out of fish bowls, on their feet all day, and privacy was limited. Buying a mobile phone means signing a credit contract, and that didn't work for customers.

'We learnt that a better option is to pick the best site, without reference to X metres at X cost, and try to negotiate on the rent,' she says. That tip shouldn't come as a surprise, and has been the common wisdom in real estate for decades: buying the worst house in the best street allows you to capitalise on your purchase. It's the potential that's important. But like everything, there are tricks along the way. 'Things like escalators,' Maxine says. 'Everyone thinks escalators are great because people use them constantly and your shop is really visible. They see you all right – but they go right past you.' And busiest is not always best, either, a point learnt by locating stores in strip locations, including one in Sydney nestled alongside one of the city's busiest streets. 'That's fine but the big question you have to ask yourself is where does a customer park?'

Despite a few hiccups, Fone Zone has been good at targeting the sweet spots in shopping centres. They've been successful because when determining the location of a new store, long hours are spent people-watching. It's something you can't do by desktop.

'You need to go out and look at it and feel it and observe the behaviour of the clients,' Maxine says. She learnt the mechanics of the ant trail at Brisbane's Toombul shopping centre, where Fone Zone was planning a trial outlet.

'I got into my car, went out there, and sat on a seat where I could see everyone,' she says. She could see the stores people rushed by, those that caused them to slow, and those that lured them in. Within hours, she could predict the path that someone parking at the front of Toombul would almost definitely take. With two options open to them, they took the same path. The window displays didn't stand out and the shop sizes varied so she could dismiss those as factors. The drawcards became obvious. Customers headed for the big retailers, many of them making that their first stop. But then once out, instead of heading back for the door, they continued on – in search of a coffee, cake, or something else. Maxine found it was the 'something else' that Fone Zone and other non-food retailers offered customers, now open to a purchase other than that they arrived to buy.

Other consumer behaviour characteristics have been learnt over time, at first through watching, and later with sophisticated demographic analysis.

'For example, women will buy more often then men and women will spend more than men,' Maxine says. 'They will pay a lot more for a haircut, they will pay way more for a blouse or a shirt. Men pay for experience. Women pay for material things and how they look.' Early on, mobile phone customers were predominantly men. Now, the company attempts to match its sales teams to the shopper. 'Let's take Bribie Island as a case in point. It's generally a retirement area, so I'd be disinclined to have some young, go-getting 20 year old there that might look or sound slightly disrespectful – although it's best not to have that in any store! But people recruit in their mirror image and they buy in their mirror image, so we need to ensure we have a range of team members in our stores.'

Over time, as networks have pursued marketing around the security mobile phones afford people and their ability to share data, they have morphed from a non-discretionary purchase to a must-buy. Even in tough economic times, there is no significant downturn in handset sales – customers are more likely to use them less, or buy fewer fashion accessories. The increase in mobile phone case sales proves the market for accessories.

'It's nothing to watch a female walk out of a store with four different cases,' Maxine says. The accessories are a response to changing consumer demands, as well as the need for mobile phone retailers to be flexible to stay profitable. Increased mobility, changing work practices and faster lifestyles have all forced contemporary changes. 'The internet has had a huge impact – on our media, our newspapers, our health and increasingly on our education. Then look at what smartphones might add to that mix. It's really interesting to watch companies that are blinkered in accepting that; they're resisting change and you know what's going to happen to them.'

So how does the internet, smartphone technology and the growing rates of online retail sales change the ant trail and how it works?

'It doesn't change the ant trail within the shopping complex,' Maxine says. 'The issue is getting them to the stores.' She gives the example of cinemas which had been removed from shopping centres, only to be reinstated. 'Shopping has to be about entertainment and centres need to cater for people who want to be social; who want to go and have a bite to eat or drink or see a movie. So our job then is to provide a reason why people will come into our store.' Telstra has found a space in educating customers who largely don't understand how to get the best out of their technology. That role is a far cry from the brick handsets of a decade ago. 'You have to keep evolving so you match those consumer behaviours. You have to be experimental. Have a go. And that's been a very clear message to my team.'

Consumer behaviours have to be considered whether you're opening a single store, or a roll-out of 85 in three and a half years – the challenge Maxine took on for Telstra towards the end of 2009. That meant around 25 stores were being opened each year. They were different sizes, in different cities and in different States; a massive undertaking that created reservations within Telstra.

Pete Connors says the locations were picked by visiting sites, not reading reports, and the Telstra agreement influenced where they went because they were representing the Telstra brand. Their current network also played a role in determining where they saw targeted points of presence. A team from Telstra and Fone Zone would sit down and nut out a plan influenced by what the carrier wanted, and where Fone Zone currently had stores. And then Pete Connors, and others, would board a plane to determine consumer behaviour in the way they always had.

'We'd go to the centre for hours and just watch. We'd then come back and do some homework on demographics. The reality is though that most of our decisions were made by being there, watching what was going on. We said "no" to more places than we said "yes" to.'

Fone Zone carried with it a 'small store mentality', so when they visited a particular centre and other people might have turned their noses up at a fit-out, or even a location, they knew – as long as it was along the ant trail – that they could make it work. Rolling out one store per month is a mammoth undertaking, with more than 120 different activities that need to be prioritised, done and run in a specific order. The 120 discrete jobs ranged from locating the store space, to designing it, fitting it out, staffing it, having all the IT issues addressed, and negotiating with landlords. Many of these tasks had to be conducted, or finished, concurrently.

The 2009 roll-outs couldn't have been more different to that of Maxine and David's first retail opening, at Pacific Fair on the Gold Coast, where the paint was still drying on opening day. Planning started with a determination of what the outcome needed to be, and then, given the short time frames, the team worked backwards. Each role in the team was decided upon and then assigned to the person responsible. That allowed people to work independently on their goal and the different aspects of the operation to run at speed – before progress was given to the project management team at regular update meetings. It developed a rhythm of its own and a store could be open for business within three months.

'It came down to teamwork, structured operating

rhythms and disciplines, and all team members staying focused,' Connors says.

The ant trail isn't the only critical factor in a roll-out: the shopping centre itself needs to be the right one. A complex geographic plan fed by demographics ranging from population to income distribution is assessed. That too needs to be flexible as the economy surges and slows, as the resources boom and bust in Queensland and Western Australia in recent years has shown.

Among the most powerful forces in retailing is the science of habit, the way our brains work to behave predictably according to how they are prompted. Author Charles Duhigg in *The Power of Habit* cites a 2006 university study that found 40 per cent of actions people performed each day weren't actions, but habits.

'At one point, we all consciously decided how much to eat and what to focus on when we got to the office, how often to have a drink or when to go for a jog,' Duhigg writes. 'Then we stopped making a choice and the behaviour became automatic. It's a natural consequence of our neurology.'

So it is in walking through shopping centres. People, like ants, have formed habits that are a powerful determinant of how they will behave – and where they will spend.

In Maxine's Words

'If you manage your footprint by desktop you will make a lot of mistakes. You can spend a lot of money to be in a big shopping centre and not be in the right location. My advice is to sit and watch, for hours, and follow the ant trail. It will rarely let you down. Likewise, remember, as with everything, you need to be flexible. You can't just put your footprint down, open a store, and decide that's where you will be for the next 20 years. Centres renovate. Other centres down the road will open up, and you need to continually and proactively manage your footprint with the aim of capturing as many customers as you can.'

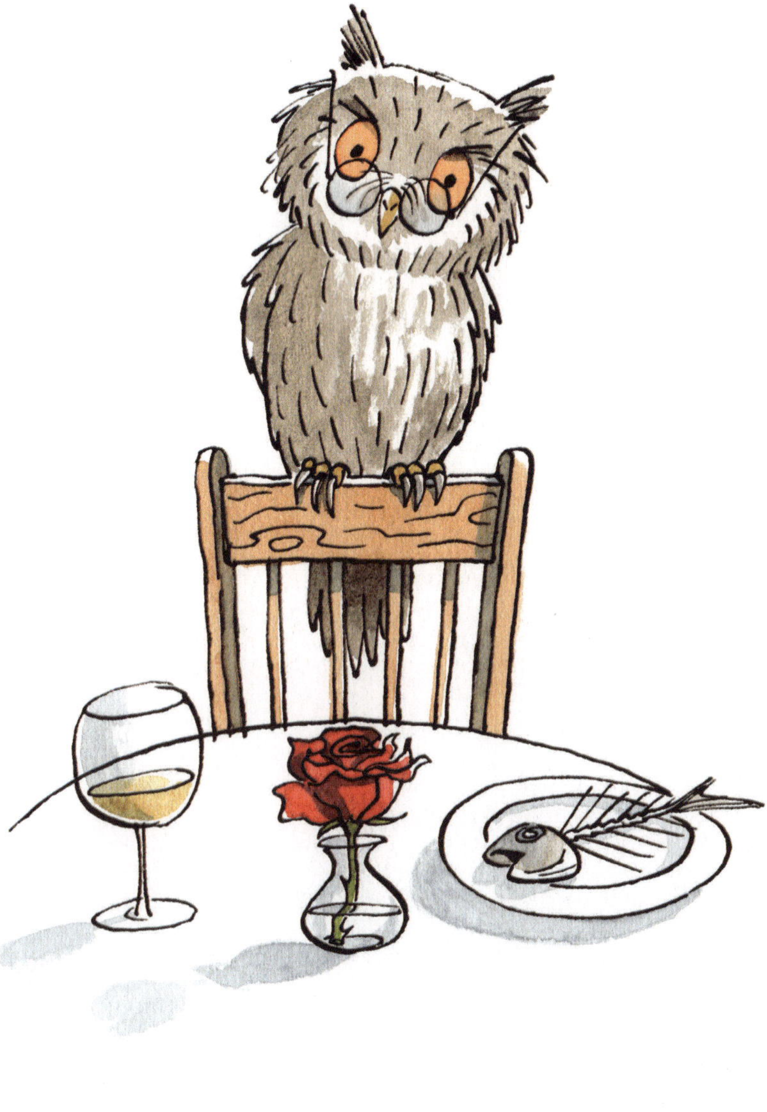

10.

Grow Yourself

'No-one saves us but ourselves. No-one can, no-one may. We ourselves must walk the path.' – Buddha

Dick Simpson picked the location well: a Sydney restaurant where it was unlikely Maxine Horne would make a scene. And he chose his words carefully, very carefully. He'd been asked to take over as chair of Vita Group, but something was holding him back. He'd been a director since September 2005 and served on the remuneration and nomination committee and the audit, compliance and risk committee. Now four years later, he was trying to decide whether he would take on the lead role. He was eminently qualified: before joining the Vita Group board, he had roles as a chief executive in both the telecommunications and computing industries. He had been the group managing director – mobiles for Telstra, chair of Hong Kong's biggest mobile carrier CSL, Telstra Clear and REACH – Asia's biggest international operator. But he was tentative about taking on this gig.

'It was about the need for Maxine to be able to change some of her behaviours, because otherwise I was not prepared to take it on,' Simpson says now. It wasn't because he didn't think she was good. 'She's a very talented, very capable, very smart individual,' he says. 'She's a prudent person. She's very focused. She brings enormous intellectual capacity to the company and thinks about it. She is a great entrepreneur and as a result of that has built a very successful business that still feels, even though it's a big business now, like a family. She is one of the most talented CEOs I have ever worked with.'

Simpson saw 'raw talent' and believed the best CEOs were not born, but made. Those who succeeded were flexible enough to learn. 'Maxine has a lovely way of looking at things, there's a mixture of humour and an incredible, almost laser-like focus where she can immediately sniff out what's bullshit and what's not,' he says. But there were a couple of ingrained character traits that he wanted to see if she would address as part of her stewardship of the company. So, over lunch, he told Maxine about a study he'd read while doing a course at the Wharton Business School in the US in 1989. In a nutshell, it showed that a person's greatest attributes could eventually become their greatest weaknesses. The careers of thousands of executives were examined to look at a phenomenon called 'derailment'. Researchers wanted to find out why some workers, who showed enormous talent and were promoted quickly, never made it to the top. 'They were meant to, they were the shining stars, but they never made it,' Simpson says. The study suggested several reasons, the predominant one being that the person's greatest strength, as they moved up the organisation, often became their greatest weakness.

To explain how the findings translate to modern managers, Simpson gives the example of a salesperson who is used to beating down every door because they will not take 'no' for an answer. They are noticed quickly.

'They are then promoted to sales manager,' he says. At this point they are given a team to lead. Goals continue to be kicked. Next stop, the team leader is made branch manager, and then onwards and upwards to the position of executive.

This is when the career trajectory can turn quickly.

'Suddenly that behaviour isn't right,' Simpson says. Where their advancement revolved around their individual effort, now the requirement is on a team effort which requires greater cooperation, more empathy, and understanding of the value a team can add. The winner-takes-all approach is no longer crucial; in fact, it can work against the manager, who finds it hard to see the big picture, rather than the next sale.

Simpson believed Maxine's greatest strength was that she was a street fighter. She liked to win, just as she had back in high school when she raced, and beat, the track star. Her background gave her that edge: a straight shooter who meant what she said, who didn't take a step back from an argument, who never gave up.

'She'd hang in there. She'd fight and claw for every inch because she doesn't like leaving anything on the table,' he says. And that helped her build the business, define a strategy for it, and make money from it. But as the company grew, and its employee team swelled, it was other qualities, Dick felt, that would determine its future. The boss had to lead by example, be conciliatory, someone who made room for partnerships. The winner-take-all approach is a common ingredient in many small businesses that begin from the bottom up. Those who have built a company from scratch have enormous skin in the game; you'll often hear them refer to their business, as Maxine often did, as their child. The public float of Fone Zone in 2005 should have cut the apron strings and allowed Maxine to take a step back. It did for a short period, but she was soon back in control and found it hard to let go. The feeling was akin to a mother saying goodbye to her 17 year old who had decided to join the army, or study at an overseas university.

That approach was the first behaviour Simpson wanted Maxine to modify. He knew it was fuelled by passion, but the CEO could not afford to refute positions on the basis they did not mirror their own. They could not always win. They needed, sometimes, to ensure something was left on the table at the end of a negotiation. Simpson wanted Maxine to see that.

There was a second trait he hoped she would address too. Maxine could become emotional and didn't care who saw it. Her anger would flare up, or she would dissolve into tears of frustration. Simpson believed that hampered her effectiveness with others because more timid staff would clam up around her. He knew that it derived from passion, but he wanted her to get the best from her team, and he thought those two behaviours were holding her back. He'd seen it in the sometimes tetchy relationship between Maxine and the board where, particularly in the early days, she had treated directors as an encumbrance. Simpson makes the point that Maxine's position was understandable. She and David had owned the company, and then, once it became public, were being questioned by directors – despite already proving they could make it a runaway success. Instead of taking a question as it was intended – perhaps even because the board was interested in her modus operandi – you could see her bristle.

Maxine understood what Simpson was saying. 'If I came across me 20 years ago I would probably strangle myself now,' she says now with disarming honesty.

Back at the Sydney restaurant table, where Simpson was contemplating taking the chair's position, Maxine sat and listened. In the nicest possible way, he got her to look into the proverbial mirror; to see the intense focus, the winner-takes-all mentality, the enormous emotion she wore on her sleeve. Simpson was looking ahead. He knew, if he could get Maxine to see the CEO she was, compared to the one she could be, there would be an immediate turnaround. And he knew that was needed to put her out to investor roadshows. Right now, over seafood and salad, he was worried that if an investor asked the wrong question, she might have 'ripped their throat out'.

He told Maxine he wanted the job, and that he thought it was a good fit. But he wanted her to learn, as part of the deal. 'I said there were some things that I believed could be improved and I was really interested to see if she was prepared to do that in my consideration of whether I was prepared to become the chair,' he says.

Maxine remembers every word of the conversation. 'I was really, really keen for him to be the chair and I was stunned at how this conversation turned round onto me! He was very good at picking his moment so he controlled the reaction – because if we had had that conversation in another room and not a restaurant, it could have ended very badly.' Maxine's gut reaction is to fight, to defend her patch and go on the attack, and that was exactly Simpson's point. But she knew he was right, and she jumped at the chance he offered for her to improve her leadership knowledge. She told him she was happy to be guided by him. He suggested an executive coach.

Executive coaches are used widely now in business,

politics, academia and in senior echelons of the public service to help leaders reach their potential. In some cases, managers use an executive coach to take the leap towards leadership. In other cases, a coach helps senior leaders build a balance between work and home. For others still, the focus might be time management. For Maxine, it was both a sounding board and the perspective it provided, and these days she arrives regularly at the office of her executive coach with a notepad ready to take pages of detail.

To change those two character traits required real personal growth. Maxine had to accept that the winner-and-loser mentality she had held for decades wasn't always best for her, or for the business. She could say it, but now she really needed to mean it. Over time, she learnt that it limited the ability of her company to forge new partnerships, and that a good negotiation, as her chair reminds her, is one where everyone leaves the table content. It would be wrong to say Maxine found it easy to change; after years and years of fighting to win, stepping back was difficult. The important thing was to moderate her behaviour. Winning was still important, so was having what she terms a 'bit of mongrel', but sometimes you had to accept that to win the war, you might need to lose a battle or two. Previously, she couldn't countenance that.

Maxine took a deliberate step back, slowly, to allow her leadership team more authority. She tried to remain seated, in the clubhouse – the leadership analogy she uses elsewhere in this book – and not get involved in every hiccup. She'd remind herself as she was stepping over the line often, and it took fits and starts, but eventually she was able to hand over more decision making to her loyal team of deputies. Its effect, while still difficult, brought results and Maxine admits that. She also knows her relationship with the board has grown exponentially as a result of her new approach. She has more time to focus on the bigger picture and to build the forward strategy, rather than the next hour's strategy.

'To be really honest, sometimes you have to take a step back and actually ask yourself whether you like the person you are becoming,' she says. 'I often ask myself that question – you know, would I like me? And if the answer is no, then I need to do something about it.'

The second personality trait that Maxine had to tame – and still does on occasion – was her propensity to show the world her emotions. If she was terribly sad, she would burst out crying; if angry, there were few in the office who were not aware of it. The Post-it note story is the perfect example. It's a reminder of another leadership attribute Maxine talks about – the shadow of a leader. In Maxine's case, an outburst of anger might last a minute, and she's forgotten it. But the person on the other end of the tirade will not have – and that casts a shadow on that relationship long after sunset.

'I think I have developed hugely over the past few years, and I had to,' Maxine says. 'I've probably also had the space to.' That last comment is a reference to the departure of David McMahon from the Vita Group and to the break-up of her marriage after almost 23 years; a sticky, hellish event around Christmas time 2012, just after the couple had finished their dream multi-million dollar Brisbane home. Maxine had been on a high, and the focus on herself was working. She had lost 23 kilograms. She had a new home. The company was powering forward. All her work, her life's work, was paying dividends. And then, bang, her marriage was over. After a protracted property settlement, David and his former PA (now his second wife) moved into the multi-million dollar home that he and Maxine had built for their family. (David McMahon declined an invitation to be interviewed for this book and has since sold that home.)

The old adage of a silver lining in every cloud has opened up the sky for Maxine though. Her colleagues say she is different. Softer, more laidback, perhaps. More empathetic. Clearer about her goals. She values time with her family and girlfriends more. And her sole stewardship of Vita Group is paying dividends.

'It was a horrendous period for her,' Dick Simpson says, 'one that required her to go deep into personal reserves of strength.' He says he has watched her grow through it. 'It challenged her enormously, was emotionally very upsetting, and a lot of learning came from that.'

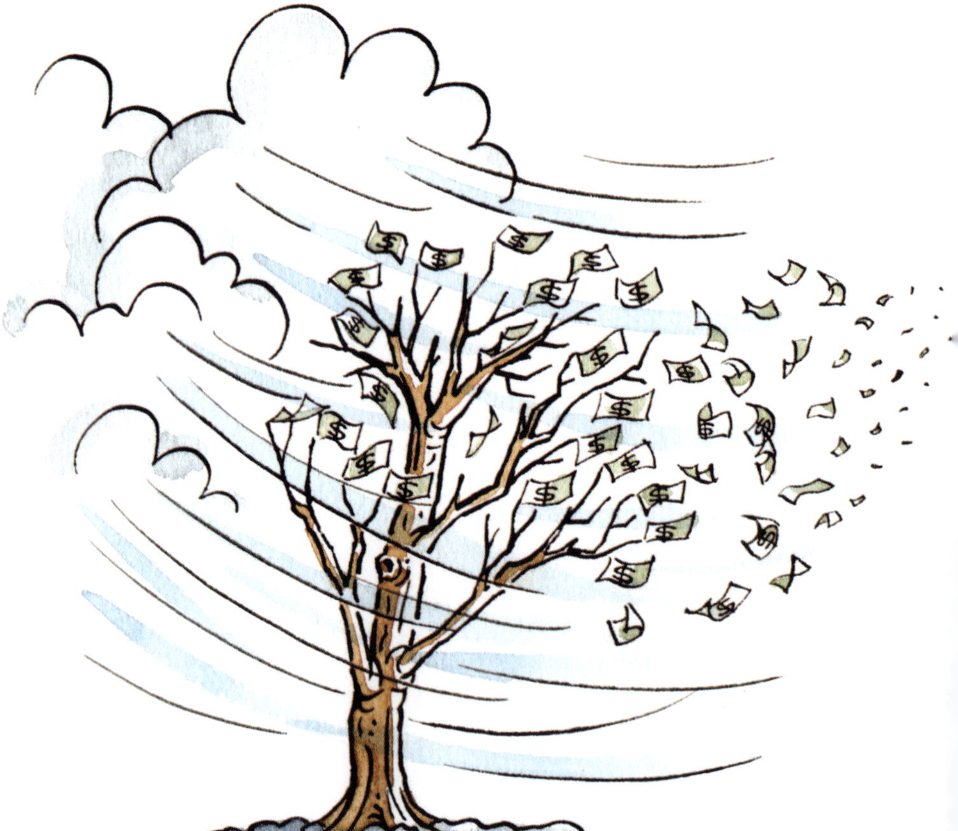

11.

Metrics Matter

'What's measured improves.' – Peter F. Drucker, Harvard Professor of Business and modern management guru

Most people will remember what they were doing when they heard Diana, Princess of Wales, died on 31 August 1997. In the same way, students of science will remember December 1995 as the month when NASA's *Galileo* probe entered Jupiter's atmosphere. Weather enthusiasts will probably recall that in the same month, the UK recorded its lowest temperature ever: −27.2 degrees Celsius in the Scottish Highlands. We remember big events through the context of what we were doing when they occurred. For

Maxine Horne, December 1995 was a time when money seemed to grow on trees, before it disappeared just as quickly. The telco industry in Australia was exploding, with a 128 per cent increase in the growth of mobile subscribers between 1993 and 1994, and a further 90 per cent increase between 1994 and 1995.

'We had a monster of a month,' Maxine says. 'It was our first December as a Telstra dealer and it was just ludicrous. As stock came in, it was flying out the door and we sat there thinking, "Wow, this is going to be amazing".'

But when the accounts finally rolled in, they told a very different story. Fone Zone had recorded a loss. 'It was so sobering,' she says. 'And I took it as a real lesson.' Two reasons were behind the scenario where a business could boast a terrific turnover but still cop a loss. First, workers were acting under directions to reach number targets which had been set further up the company chain. This meant that instead of working to gross profit goals, they were being told to sell 500 phones, for example. In order to achieve those numbers, they were giving accessories away, cutting the price on deals, and doing whatever it took to reach the targets.

Second, it was Maxine and David's first Christmas in retail and, as any small business knows, that can bring enormous challenges. For example, the importance of a roster system, and the need for increased staff and allowance for penalty rates escaped Maxine and David's attention. Costs ran up as quickly as turnover. 'We just couldn't believe it and we walked away determined that we would never allow it to happen again. You cannot – and here is the lesson – manage a business just on top line sales.'

Of course, if revenue lines are up and a business is doing what it should elsewhere, money will eventually flow to the bottom line. But Maxine's emphasis was on driving sales at the expense of everything else. Each night, stores would fax through details of all transactions which would be collated on a spreadsheet. Stores would then be given sales rankings. It was one-dimensional and didn't address the whys – why a store might be performing below others, or why a particular salesperson was unable to translate a conversation with a customer into a sale. Maxine knows now that that was a mistake, but she also knows that in a huge growth industry, the odd mistake doesn't crucify you.

'If you made that mistake today, it would all be over. The lesson was this: you don't just manage a business through the top line, you have to manage the whole profit and loss statement.'

December 1995 prompted serious discussion within Vita Group as to how it could differentiate itself from others in a growth industry. Not long after, those discussions would lead to a serious and targeted effort at customer care.

But another lesson lay hidden in the figures of December 1995. Team members were being given direction on what to do – that is, to sell a certain number of handsets – but at no stage were they hand-held during the process. They were not being taught how to do it. That was judged, in a fairly unscientific way by today's standards, by mystery shoppers.

'Coming from a sales background I am very used to allocating a target and measuring the progress, monitoring what is going on, putting out sales ladders and saying, yes, here's your commission,' Maxine says. 'So how do you do that when it's not a physical number?' The mystery shoppers were employed by a third company to act as paying customers. They would then use the transaction to study the behaviour behind a sale or a non-sale. 'We weren't interested in the sale because we could get that from the numbers being faxed through to us,' Maxine says. 'What we were interested in was the actual experience. So we worked quite closely with a mystery shopping company and we would give people money because we didn't want them to turn up and go through the process but not actually buy something.'

Mystery shoppers would buy a handset and have Telstra connect it. It would then be disconnected without penalty. This prevented sales teams from suspecting a mystery shopper. Every store was mystery-shopped, with bonuses handed out to the store or business manager when 80 per cent of customer 'interactions' by team members scored a mark higher than eight out of 10. This meant that the customer service program was being monitored.

'I laugh now about these modern ways of checking

on customer interaction – like the net promoter score,' Maxine says, referring to the means of tracking customer satisfaction (or advocacy as it's known now), 'because we were doing just that back in 1996. And the reason is simple. What gets measured, monitored and rewarded gets done.'

Maxine repeats that adage often. Measure. Monitor. Reward. 'You've got to have those three things because, otherwise, you will launch something and it will naturally die a death because no-one is driving and monitoring it.'

The method of both measurement and monitoring results, circa 2016, is entirely different, as it has changed and become more sophisticated at regular intervals since 1996. For starters, everyone is now motivated on profit not volume. That itself was not an easy reform.

'When we first did that I had people saying it was a mistake because individual team members would know how much we made on each product and they might tell someone else. But I didn't care about that. What damage can be done there? Customers know we are in the business to make money – and one of our specific values goes to that – we are proud to be profitable as profitability equals opportunity.' This point sets Vita Group apart from many other businesses where information is often the domain of the management group. That is not the case here, and salespeople in stores across the country have access to a wide variety of data.

Despite the huge sales in December 1995, Maxine and David had not made any profit. 'I learnt that if I need my people to be focused on the profit, they actually have to know how to get there – and that makes a big difference,' Maxine says. 'So the commission structures are all based on profit and they know that if they are not selling the right thing then they are not going to hit their numbers.' (Commission structures are not capped, allowing team members to receive more than 100 per cent of their salary.) The upshot is that KPIs are not just built around profit; they include customer service goals. At the store level, business managers face the same system. Indeed, a set of four KPIs envelops the whole team, whether they're on the retail floor, or in the back office supporting retail activity. They sit under four umbrellas – sales and profit, people, customer experience and efficient tools and process.

A sophisticated software program now collates information central to those KPIs daily. Online journals that are system-generated are delivered to team members via tablets. They then use them to chronicle their day – from sales to goals to coaching. The information it provides gives area managers, the leadership team and particularly the chief operating officer Pete Connors a wealth of data – and it's a joke among team members that he spends his time, late into the night in bed, checking up on stores. Each morning, though, a manager – or the chief operating officer – is able to contact a specific store about an issue. The information can show what each store's sales figures are like, how that compares to conversation rates, whether they have been able to add any 'attachments' to the sales, and where they sit next to budget, and next to other stores in other States.

Importantly, these metrics highlight trends in particular models and attachments. But they also show something else, which addresses one of the lessons from the December 1995 experience. The information rolls up from store level, to area level, State and regional level, allowing the leadership team to compare different stores, team members, leaders and the coaching that has been done. In addition to showing sales, it allows the company to support individuals who might be struggling. For example, if salesperson X has not been successful despite dealing with several customers, something is not working. That would provide a flag to a manager to see how many 'sales coaching lessons' the employee had undertaken, how he or she had performed at those, and whether there had been any change in performance between them. Those internal metrics are then added to by follow-up that customers receive that measure how likely they would be to return, and recommend others.

'It means that we can now get incredible detail on what customers say about particular salespeople and what the trends are around that store, or State, and even that day of the week,' Maxine says.

The genesis for the current system lies in work done a decade ago by two employees – Wayne Smith and Kendra Hammond – who along with Maxine worked on a performance, review and feedback system for all team members.

'Not only was it focused on what they were doing, but it also brought in the dimension of how they did it,' Hammond says. Values were built into the process and a system developed to pinpoint the behavioural attributes that would signal adherence to individual values. 'We came up with a set of behaviours for leaders and a set of behaviours for team members that we'd look for them to be displaying.'

Wayne Smith says enormous effort was ploughed into ensuring a link between culture, values and performance. 'Everyone was clear about the objectives of their role and how their leaders set their job plans and assessed those, and we had a performance assessment process that incorporated the what and the how. You either achieved your sales targets or you didn't, and then we assessed people against those values. Salary increases and bonuses were linked to the demonstration of Vita Group's values. That was an example of how we were significantly looking to impact the culture without actually talking about it.'

Maxine believes analysing metrics provides an opportunity to boost the performance of eight out of every 10 sales staff. This view is canvassed and explained elsewhere in this book, but in short, 10 per cent of sales staff – despite the effort put in – will always succeed. A further 10 per cent are likely to sit at the bottom, despite any amount of coaching. The big chunk of sales teams sits in the middle – representing eight in every 10 team members.

'The way to improve your bottom line is to improve the performance of that big group in the middle,' Maxine says. 'By increasing their performance by five per cent you'll see a big financial increase.'

Non-performers who come under the metrics spotlight are subject to further targeted coaching, which focuses on 'their mindset, actions and behaviours' before their results are monitored again. If it doesn't then change, they have to leave the business.

'I come back to this fact, though: there are only two reasons why people don't do things – will or skill,' Maxine says. 'So first, we address the skill. Have they done each one of their training modules? Have they been quizzed on them? Has the business manager or area manager tasked with their care tried to get them up to speed and how have they gone about that? We make sure we go down the coaching path – but in the end they may not be suited to the business. People don't turn up to work thinking, "I am going to do a crappy job today". Something happens, and most of the time it's either system-driven, process-driven or leader-driven. Those are the three factors. We have to find out why – whether it's a result of a system failure or a process failure or whether the leader in that area requires some attention – and then fix it.'

Maxine no longer focuses on individual store sales reports, but on monthly and annual sales comparisons, and manages by exception. The minute analysis is left to her leadership team. 'But, and here's another lesson, we find that nine times out of 10 if there is a problem in a particular store not performing, you can link that back to the store leader,' she says.

The use of metrics is loved in some companies and not in others. Vita Group loves them, but their use will always prompt debate because a level of judgement is required, and in the case of Vita Group, metrics are used to weight behaviours versus output. So far, the belief is that the four KPIs that envelop all jobs – profitability and growth; people and culture; customer and community engagement; effective tools and processes – work well in recognising high achievers and targeting others for assistance. But whatever tweaks occur over time, non-financial measures will always rate highly.

'You have to actually do the activities to get the financial outcome,' Maxine says. 'And they need to be checked and measured. We consciously made the decision years ago that if we get our people right, the customers will come, and from there sales and profit will follow.'

In Maxine's Words

Q. How much focus do you put on measuring performance?

A. Everybody in this business gets measured and monitored like you wouldn't believe. When I do interviews I say we polarise people and you either love working for us or you hate it. There is nowhere to hide. I can call up a store in Western Australia and see what a sales consultant is doing. I can see how many customers they have served, what their average transaction was and what they sold them.

Q. How is it done?

A. We use software that has been designed internally. It has evolved over the years as business requirements have evolved. I'm proud of our ability to see something we need, and then address it.

Q. Why the focus?

A. What gets measured, monitored and rewarded gets done. In order to achieve something, nothing in this business happens unless we've got monitoring in place and remuneration against it and that remuneration may be a reward or it might be monetary.

Q. If you could talk to your 19-year-old self about how you are doing your job, would you have done it the same or differently?

A. I would have been a lot more disciplined – in my head at 19 I thought that salespeople were born and they are not, they're made. You might have natural characteristics and you might enjoy speaking to people but good salespeople are made. They are not born.

Q. What is the best quality a salesperson can have?

A. Being able to listen, and understand what is important to the customer.

Q. You run the company – do you still see yourself as a salesperson?

A. Whenever I travel and I come back into the country and they ask what your occupation is, I put 'sales', because that's what I am. I sell my business, to the market, to customers, and I sell it to our team to keep them in the business.

Q. What's the genesis of your belief that every role should be able to be measured?

A. Essentially it came from my sales days. We've expanded it considerably over the years, but when you work in sales, your job is to make sales. When I was working in the UK, there was an expectation that three months of missed sales meant you were under a lot of pressure. Some people put the pressure on themselves to make budget in those three months or they expected they would be finding a new job. Now, we can measure things to get a better idea of what's really happening.

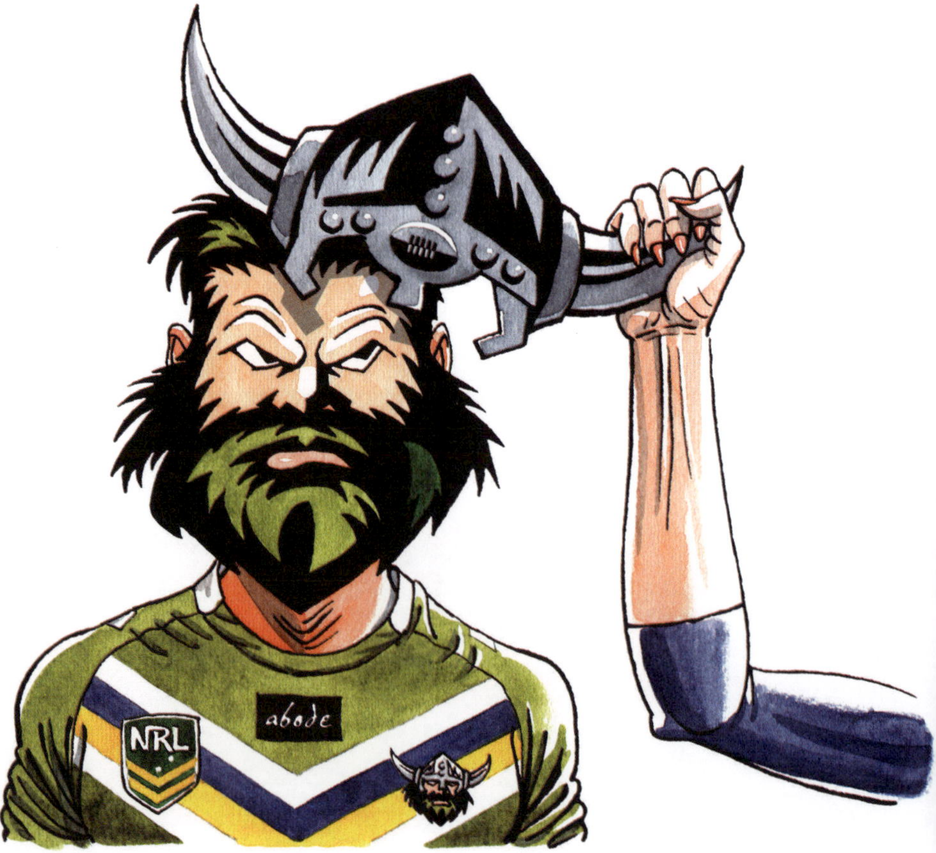
NRL
abode

12.

Put Value in Values

'At the end of the day, the position is just a position, a title is just a title and those things come and go. It's really your essence and your values that are important.' – Queen Rania of Jordan

Maxine grabbed a glass of wine and walked into the lounge room. It had been another long day and her husband David McMahon was engrossed in a rugby league game on TV. It was the winter of 2002 and the Canberra Raiders were having a scrap.

Maxine sat down. 'Why don't they have anything on their shirts?' she asked David. The Raiders were at the top of the league table at the time, but they couldn't snag a sponsor. 'We should sponsor them.'

The following Monday morning, she called Raiders' headquarters and three days later, club heavyweights Mal Meninga and Don Furner were sitting across the table from Maxine and David in Brisbane, happily signing a three-year deal. The impetus, on Fone Zone's part, was to get the brand into lounge rooms across Australia. A bit of ego contributed to the decision; the idea that they could do it appealed too. In retrospect, it didn't translate into a profitable arrangement, at least in marketing terms. But one of the values Maxine adopted for her own company came from the mouth of Raiders' head coach Matthew Elliott.

'We went down and had a tour of the clubhouse and we were walking around the dressing rooms and we met with Matthew Elliott,' Maxine says. David asked how he had turned the team around. The Raiders' head coach between 2001 and 2006 spoke about the importance of teamwork and how decisions were made. Maxine's interest piqued.

Later, Elliott gave a speech to Maxine and David's team. 'Every decision I make and every decision made in the organisation is not about individuals,' he said. 'All the decisions are made on the team coming first.' It was a mantra the team had heard Elliott mention often, but Maxine loved it. It now is plastered across the wall inside the reception of Vita Group's Brisbane support centre. Every Action is taken with the Whole Team in Mind.

While Matthew Elliott was the inspiration for that particular value, Maxine's early life, and the role played by her grandparents, are the impetus for many others. Maxine's childhood was unpropitious, as evidenced by the old tins that sat in the bottom of her grandmother's cupboard. Each had a distinct purpose and Maxine can remember the tin that was marked for electricity. Another was for food. Each week, her grandparents would divide their earnings between tins, always worried they'd come up short. It wasn't the only illustration of their frugality. The joint of meat which had pride of place at Sunday dinner was then used for the rest of the week: one night it would be Cornish pasties, toad-in-the-hole on another, and sandwiches on a third. The vegies came from their little garden in the backyard.

'I'm a saver now,' Maxine says. 'I hate taking money out of a non-bank ATM because it charges $2!' It wasn't only the imperative of saving that her grandparents taught a young Maxine. They provided the inspiration for many of the values that now adorn the wall in Vita Group's reception.

1. Our people and customers are everything to us

This heads the list of values and was the one articulated first, back in 1996. Even today, team members are told it, repeatedly, from day one. It's the basis for the company's CARE (Customers Are Really Everything) program, and the point of difference Maxine believes her company offers. 'And I've learnt my lesson here,' she says. 'During the GFC we cut back on some of those little things we do for customers – like getting them a coffee if they have to wait too long. Cutting back was a mistake, and I wouldn't do it again.'

2. Every action is taken with the benefit of the whole team in mind

This is taken from Matthew Elliott's speech soon after Fone Zone began sponsoring the Canberra Raiders. Elliott, who now runs corporate culture programs, says it is equally applicable in business as it is in a football team. 'Some people in leadership don't have the skills to engage their staff,' he says. 'They think teamwork is about how they work together rather than communicating, engaging and connecting.'

3. The collective wisdom and effort of the team always outperforms the individual

Maxine's chief operating officer Pete Connors decided on this one, and teamwork is encouraged from store level to management level. But it goes further than that. Vita Group actively employs those that show they have runs on the board in a team environment. 'In a big organisation, everyone has to work together to get the best possible result and if someone is out of step with that it stands out,' Maxine says. 'They'll have trouble dealing with their peers, and trouble managing both up and down the line. Sometimes I think teamwork is underrated.' The stimulus for this value was in the silos that formed as the business grew. It's not a unique problem, and technology now helps forge partnerships between different parts, whether it is a government department or a financial corporation. Vita Group decided to combat the silo phenomena through cross-functional teams that come into operation as soon as a particular program or project needs to be rolled out. 'Over the years we have moved from having great individuals to having great teams, and for me that's important,' Maxine says. The best example of this was the roll-out of 85 Telstra stores in just over three years; a mammoth effort which meant a new store being opened weekly, at some stages.

4. You get what you work for

Maxine spent her childhood in a three-bedroom semi-detached council house in Ipswich in the UK. It was working class to the bootstraps. Her grandparents, who became her carers after her parents split, couldn't afford many luxuries, and Maxine learnt the value of what was important. She remembers how she and her younger sister Michelle would receive rare visits from their mother, and longer but irregular visits from their father. Her grandparents, who were married for 65 years, lived a simple life, putting her to bed each night, making sure she had enough to eat, and working long days. Her grandfather George was a carpenter and would often escape to the little shed in his garden. Her grandmother Rose was a cleaner in the local pub. Life was hard, and Maxine felt a bit like a pawn in an adult game waged by her parents. But her grandparents shielded her as best they could, despite the propensity of young children to ask question after question after question. Maxine remembers the little shed which brought her grandfather joy almost every afternoon. 'I was only young – probably eight or nine – and I remember him sitting there, asking me when I was going to start work.'

5. We're proud to be profitable as profitability equals opportunity

In a list of values that encourages team members to feel good and act well, this one might jar. Make a profit. Be proud of the profit. 'In the early days, I was a little bit embarrassed about the money and I didn't want to talk about it,' Maxine says. 'But I realised that in order to engage people, they need to understand that we are running a business – and businesses need to be profitable.' Maxine says shareholders are often used as the rationale for creating a business that boasts a healthy profit, but there was a greater imperative to be successful. 'If we aren't profitable, we're not going to be here and team members won't have a job. We've got to be able to create opportunity for our people.' That means profitability is talked about, at all levels, regularly. Every business unit in the company has a P&L and every leader is required to 'own' that P&L. They are trained in being business owners, taught how to run a P&L, how to manage balance sheets and cash flows, and they get a profit share on their P&L. Sophisticated metrics, which are discussed elsewhere in this book, are used to track individual store 'businesses' in real time, and profitability sits with personal performance measures as barometers of individuals' successes. 'We have a whole heap of KPIs across people's performance plans in a way we never did, early on. I really believe that if you can't KPI a role, then you shouldn't have it in the first place.'

6. Dare to be different as creativity drives innovation

This is really about establishing a point of difference, or in the case of Vita Group, celebrating its quirkiness. 'When people ask me to describe the business I always say that we are a little bit left of centre,' Maxine says. 'We're not exactly normal, but probably not abnormal either. Just a bit different.' That position is intentional, as is the specific use of the word 'creativity'. 'Creativity doesn't mean that you've invented the spaceship that will travel to the moon – it means that you've taken a very difficult process and made it simple, or that you've added value to something by thinking outside the square, or coming to it from another angle. We encourage people to do that.' Vita Group has a complex cascading awards and recognition system to acknowledge those employees who come up with an idea that ends up being implemented. 'I'd like to think this business isn't about me or any one person,' Maxine says. 'It's about everybody.' Leaders are encouraged to create a 'VIBE' – a Vibrant Innovative Business Environment, the foundation term for the company's culture – for both their teams and their customers.

7. Always do the right thing

'My grandfather would always say this too,' Maxine says. 'Always do what you believe is right. You know when you've done something wrong so I say to people they don't need me to tell them. They know it.' She gives the example of her grandfather providing for her grandmother during World War II. Her grandmother Rose never left the UK. Her grandfather's only trip abroad was in World War II when he was a signalman in the 8th army. He was captured in Italy but escaped. Re-captured, he managed to escape a second time. Rose was told he was missing in action. She knew he wasn't. 'He didn't go back to his outfit so he joined a group of Americans and spent the remainder of the war with them,' Maxine says. She remembers as a nine year old hearing her grandfather relay another of his war stories. 'Every week a van would come in and allocate them new uniforms. They'd have a shower and be given soap, stockings and chocolate.' George would use the soap, but the stockings and chocolates would always find their way home to his beloved Rose. 'And that's why she knew he was alive. She knew he would always do the right thing – and that was both making sure she shared his luxuries and knowing he wasn't dead.'

8. Love what you do

No other value matches Maxine's personality quite like this. 'If you aren't passionate about working here, then don't,' she says. 'If someone is miserable they're going to make their team miserable and that means they'll make our customers miserable. Life's too short, and it's just not worth it. I say go and find something that you love, that you have a passion for, and something that you really want to do. I want people to really want to be here. I've been forced to have conversations with employees on this and I've said to them, "You are clearly not happy, why don't you take two weeks' leave and go and find another job because it's no use being here and not enjoying it".' Maxine found her passion working for Mercury Communications, under Tricia Mittens, in the UK. While she started at Barclays Bank, she always had an eye out for the job that would provide her with passion. Accepted into the West Merseyside Police, she declined. Accepted into the army, she declined. Accepted into university to study physical education, she declined. She was just marking time until she found something that drove her passion. 'It should be the same with anyone who works here. If it's a fit, that's super. But if it's not, they are better off somewhere where they really want to be.'

These eight values underpin everyday conversations and form part the foundation for decision making at Vita Group. But it hasn't always been that way. For a long time, the values resided in Maxine's head. She knew what she wanted and expected that, in some way, it would be transferred to those who worked with her.

'But I didn't really articulate it to our people early on and that was a big mistake and one I'd urge others not to make,' she says. 'I should have done it from day one.' But once she had, she stuck by it.

Kendra Hammond, who joined Fone Zone as organisational development manager in 2007, once suggested the values could be altered slightly, perhaps so they were more easily understood. 'And Maxine said you don't f... with the values,' Hammond says now. 'It struck me that they were sacred. These are what she lived and reinforced every single day. It was very clear to me that we weren't going to be messing with them.'

Maxine says the values fit the personal life of her leadership team, her own children, and many of her employees. 'Think about it. As a parent, these are core values that you really want your kids to feel. You get what you work for. Make the right decisions. Do what you love. Aren't those a good creed for everyday living?'

Luke Wadeson began work in 2002 as a part-time salesman at Chermside in Brisbane. Fourteen years later, he is one of the company's best performers.

'The thing that always sticks with me is that Maxine consistently highlights our core values,' he says. 'It's what I live by. I'm a walking, talking version of our core values.' Luke, like other young workers, nominates Maxine as one of the biggest influences in his life. 'I've had a few stern talking-tos. At the end of the day, VIBE is just an acronym and core values are just words, but without a leader who truly believes and lives them, they mean nothing.'

In The Words Of Others

'This is the first company I've worked for,' Andrew Leyden says, 'where the values really matter and everyone uses them.' He gives the example of an employee performance review where more time is spent on adherence to the values and the behaviour of the employee than what they have achieved in terms of sales. 'All companies say they have values but not all of them demonstrate and care about them. And the reason I'm still here is the environment that Maxine creates – you can have fun, think freely, share your views openly, where you don't have to worry too much about politics.'

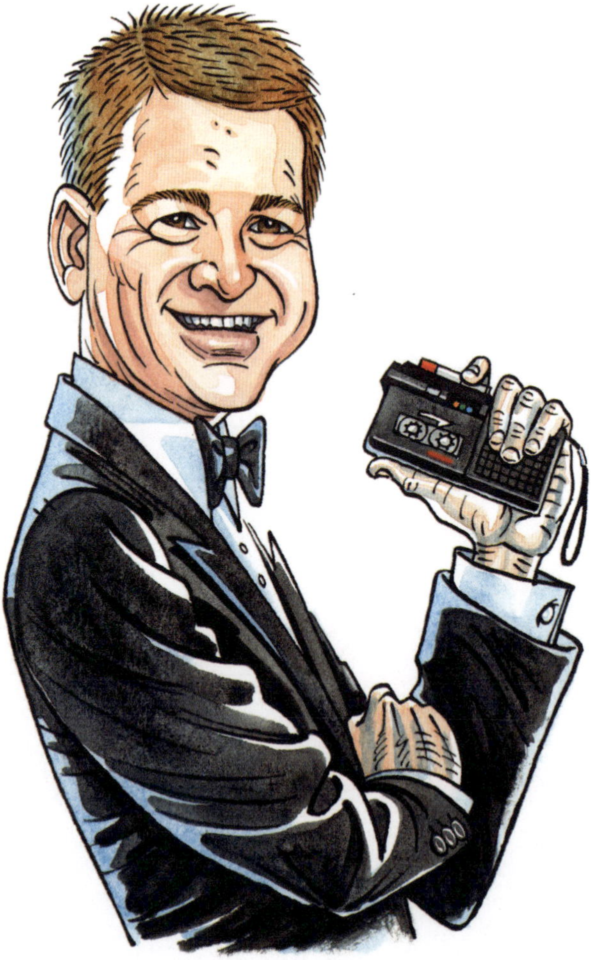

13.

Give Diligence its Due

'If you are going through hell, keep going.' – Sir Winston Churchill, former British Prime Minister

It was August 1996, and Maxine and David were driving back from a trip to the Gold Coast. Out of the blue, the spectacularly sunny day was pierced by a phone call from their new business partner. 'Jump on a plane,' David recalls hearing. 'What airport are you the nearest to? Jump on a plane, get down here.' The new business partner was phoning from Melbourne but planned to be in Sydney the next day. Could they meet? David said he'd book a flight.

Maxine was tired. She'd spent the morning in their Robina store, but something about the phone call panicked her. She could only hear snippets, but a sense of foreboding overcame her; that indescribable feeling in the pit of your stomach when you know something isn't right.

She turned to David, who was driving the car. 'Let's stop and buy a tape recorder,' she said. 'I want you to tape the conversation because I don't believe what's happening.'

The voice on the other end of the line was Sean Whitsen [name changed for legal reasons], a director of the Interact Group, a handful of companies that boasted $65 million turnover. Two months earlier, Maxine and David had agreed to sell Fone Zone Pty Ltd to Interact. It wasn't a flash-in-the-pan decision; David had undertaken negotiations over a couple of months and they both believed they had made a small fortune and could now move on. Neither of them gave much attention to what they would do next, but in the short term, they'd continue to run the new business. Other decisions could wait and, with a price tag of $1.75 million, they had signed on the dotted line in June 1996. At this point in time possession and control of the Fone Zone business had passed to the Interact Group pending completion. In signing the deal, and parting with possession prior to settlement, Maxine and David had placed their future in the hands of Interact.

They knew before that phone call in August that the

new venture was in trouble; on 1 July they had expected the $157,000 deposit from the sale to turn up in their bank account. It didn't. Several weeks earlier, Maxine and David had attended another meeting in Melbourne. They left knowing financial difficulties were enveloping the new enterprise after an expected equity injection failed to materialise.

So on the drive back to Brisbane from the Gold Coast that sunny afternoon, they stopped and purchased a small tape recorder.

The next day, Thursday, 22 August 1996, David and Sean, Interact-Fone Zone Pty Ltd director, met in the Ansett Golden Wing Lounge at Sydney.

David McMahon: 'How are you doing?'
Sean Whitsen: 'Good. You? Shall we grab a room?'
David McMahon: 'Have you got one booked?'
Sean Whitsen: 'Oh, we'll just go in this one.'
David McMahon: 'I'm sure they'll throw us out if they need it.'
Sean Whitsen: 'Would you like a cup of coffee?'
David McMahon: 'No, I'm okay. I've just had some stuff on the plane.'

Both men then moved into the conference room, the small recording machine taping every word.

'To this day,' Maxine says now, 'I'm not quite sure why I was so emphatic about stopping and buying that tape recorder. But I'm so glad we did. In an episode where we did so much wrong, that was one thing we did really right. But this whole lesson comes down to due diligence, and how you see partnerships, and ensuring your brand, in any partnership, is matched with a brand of similar values and culture. This agreement wasn't right from the word go, but we went into it feet first. Perhaps it was out of naivety, perhaps it was the lure of realising our fortune, or perhaps we were keen on growing the businesses and thought this was the only way to do it …'

Back in the Golden Wing Lounge meeting room, which had now been booked for the next hour, the conversation between Sean Whitsen and David McMahon continued.

Sean Whitsen: 'The business is f...ed. I guess you've been working that out over the last couple of weeks. We're totally, we're totally stuffed and … the thing that has dragged us down is retail.'

The men continued to talk about where the business was going and how they might escape the problems. At one stage David left the room to go to the bathroom, rewound the tape to where he left off, checked it, and walked back into the room.

The lack of trust in this story is palpable, and it's hard to imagine a venture being successful when so much doubt fills the relationship. That distrust only grew, when the parties ended up in protracted legal fights, beginning a week later when Maxine and David told Interact-

Fone Zone Pty Ltd's solicitors that they considered them in breach of the agreement they'd signed and were terminating it. As Supreme Court injunctions unfolded, along with a Supreme Court case appraisal, almost everything became the subject of dispute, and claim and counter-claim revolved around monies owed, uniforms, Telstra connections, payments, stock and responsibility.

The fractious relationship only worsened 10 days after the Ansett Golden Wing Lounge conversation when Maxine and David tried to retake control of the business. They hatched a bold plan: David travelled to Melbourne, a senior employee caught a plane to Sydney and headed to the western suburbs, while Maxine remained in Queensland. Simultaneously, they asked their entire workforce to resign, without giving notice, but to continue to turn up to work.

'We brought everyone together and we told them the truth,' Maxine says. That truth was that they had made a terrible mistake and were facing ruin. Jobs would be lost and no-one would walk away with a smile. But they had one ace up their sleeve. They still legally owned the bricks and mortar stores by virtue of a charge (akin to a caveat being put over a property sale) recommended by their lawyer which crystallised once Interact defaulted. They told workers that they were going to fight to get the business back. This was an audacious bid. It was Friday afternoon.

'We cannot employ you legally or permanently until Monday,' Maxine remembers telling a store full of team members in Brisbane, 'but we can employ you on a casual basis over the weekend. If you come with us, it's going to be hard. Really hard.' She says they decided to be transparent and open, telling the staff they only had limited stock and not much more in the bank. 'We are going to have to trade out of this,' she said. She was banking on workers understanding how perilous the situation was, not only for Maxine and David's stake in a business, but their own employment. This could have proved a high-risk move. Workers could have walked out, or not turned up for the next shift. But they knew they had no choice but to attempt to take the business back and trade out of their problems. Maxine and David had worked on a script before addressing staff, who were told there would be no pay rises for about three years. 'But if you stay, we'll get through this,' she ended. 'And I'd love you to do that.'

Maxine says only a few of the sales team didn't then turn up. 'They showed up, one by one, for every shift in every store all weekend. I would say that it is the proudest moment I have experienced. I talked to all these salespeople, the team, telling them exactly how it is – and they still kept turning up for work.'

That sense of success was short-lived though. Within days, Interact Group had struck back and lodged an injunction and further legal claims against David, Maxine and Fone Zone. That triggered a flurry of legal actions which sat like a shadow over them, and the business, for more than two years.

The lessons that flowed from this episode, at least for Maxine, are numerous, and one suggests for the other side too. Sean Whitsen was certainly surprised and caught off-guard to learn later that he had been secretly recorded by David. He declined an invitation to be interviewed for this book.

Trust features highly on that list of lessons. A manager must be able to trust his or her team members. A CEO must be able to trust his or her leadership team. Trust between a board and an executive needs to be comprehensive. So does trust between partners or, as this case showed, it will not work. Listening to expert advice is crucial. Maxine and David had already learnt that lesson and had a financial controller Shiu Chand on board. But it was another piece of advice, provided by their lawyer, that helped them navigate their way out of this action. The lawyer had suggested that they keep a charge over the assets of their business, preventing them from being sold. To this day, Maxine is grateful she took that advice.

'He kept asking us whether we wanted to go ahead with the deal. He was being cautious, and we just jumped in and said everything would be fine. That's when he told us – insisted really – that a charge be held over the assets until all monies were paid. I will always remember that and be forever grateful. If ever I needed proof that expert advice is needed, that was it. An expert, at your side, is on your team, and it's an important addition to any business.'

'Trust and a willingness to take expert advice weren't the only lessons. I think I learnt to slow down too. So much in life is about timing: when you get married, when you have children, when you start your own business, when you decide to branch out, when you grow via greenfields and when you might embark on an acquisition plan – all those issues require you to look at the timing. And we didn't. We thought we'd hit the jackpot, and dived in, boots and all.'

New parents are often advised to get down on their hands and knees and crawl around their home. The aim of the exercise is to see the risk factors that might not be obvious from lofty heights: the power sockets, a small glass drawer at the bottom of the cabinet or the broken spring that sticks out under the bed. None of those are dangerous to an adult; but all could seriously hurt a baby who has just learnt to crawl. Due diligence is no different, and if you had to encapsulate what went wrong for Maxine and David in this venture, it comes down to those two words. Due diligence.

Due diligence determines whether a plan fits. This didn't. In fact, it really only fitted Maxine and David's plan to make money and even that was questionable. Due diligence requires a view over the next hill. What risks are hiding ahead? And how do I calculate them? Risk management is part and parcel of any business, and the structure needs to be developed with that in mind.

'To put it into context, we really didn't have a huge management structure then as well,' Maxine says. 'We'd been flogging our butts, we weren't taking any dividend, because we didn't know what a dividend policy was, and we saw selling as our way to make money. So we went into this deal with no due diligence whatsoever.' That means no risks were identified or measured and Maxine and David spent no time considering their risk tolerance. The decision to sell the business was taken at face value after a couple of months of negotiation.

'It's really important to look at the person or the business you are dealing with, and that should be done early on, and certainly before ink is attached to any deal,' she says. 'I know it was that little tape recorder that saved us. But the fact that we had it showed the lack of trust, and showed that we had not looked at this deal properly in the first place.'

Financially, it meant lean times ahead. 'I felt really ashamed,' she said. 'I can remember one day walking past a former team member who was selling fruit cakes for a charity and getting really angry. I couldn't on some days see our way out of it. There was a huge amount of stress. And it was our fault for not really being on top of things at the beginning.'

Three years later, in 2000, the business was growing again. But a hard lesson in due diligence had been learnt. Later, with another big purchase, it had to be relearnt. But those other lessons proved valuable too. Preparation: buying that tape recorder. Using your gut instinct.

'If something doesn't smell right, it probably isn't. If it doesn't feel right, then it's probably not,' Maxine says.

Do you trust who you are dealing with? 'Whether it's within your team or outside, there is a big problem if trust doesn't exist. Get rid of the distrust, or get rid of the relationship, because it is only going to end up bad.' And of course, listen to your advisers. 'One of the things that I always say to people now is that if that's the advice, why aren't we following it? I mean, if you pay all this money for an expert opinion, there's got to be a good reason why you would then turn your back on it.'

The Interact episode is also a reminder of the importance of engaging your workforce. The decision by most to stay on – which in many cases would have been an economic imperative – allowed Fone Zone's profits to ring loud again later. But the biggest lesson, at least for Maxine, is that due diligence is needed for a very, very good reason.

'We were on the verge of losing our home, the business, everything – and it was no-one else's fault but our own. The buck stopped with us.'

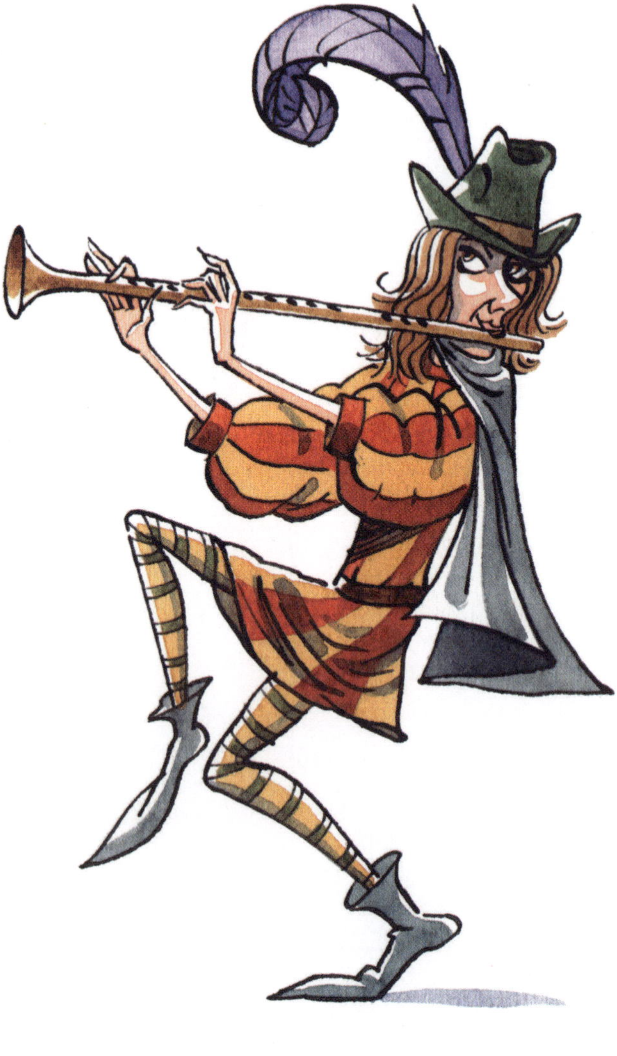

14.

Put the Cult into Culture

'Culture eats strategy for breakfast.' – Peter F. Drucker, Harvard Business School professor and guru of modern management

The Pike Place Fish Market in Seattle, US, is a sight to behold and known in business circles the world over. It wasn't always the case though; it teetered on bankruptcy just 30 years ago. Today, it attracts more than 10,000 visitors every day in what has been a remarkable turnaround. The story, which is the subject of documentaries, books and motivational talks, goes along these lines. The market was purchased by John Yokoyama, an employee, five

Lessons in business leadership from **Maxine Horne**

decades ago. Later, when its financial statements were bathed in red, meetings were held to try and nut out a plan to win back customers, and perhaps even find a few new ones. Someone piped up with a suggestion that they think big and make the market famous the world over. People would come for the theatre and leave with dinner, and they would return time and time again to see the attitude of staff, to watch the games where fish are thrown around the market, and where they, as customers, could be chased by staff carrying a monkfish, or a giant octopus. It's been perfected over time. But that gem of an idea turned the Pike Place Fish Market into a phenomenal business that now includes calendars, gift cards, shot glasses, motivational speeches and shopping bags, photo galleries, books and a fish cam. And in the process, it's become the inspiration for businesses the world over looking for that dash of energy that will energise both staff and the bottom line.

John Weir was working for Maxine as head of human resources in the late 1990s when she needed help in taking the culture she wanted out of her head and onto paper. She wanted a culture that wasn't scripted but encouraged people to be respectful, to take their work seriously, but be able to poke fun at themselves along the way. This was at the point where Maxine was the mother of a toddler, and exhausted, trying to find a light at the end of a long, long tunnel. The business was growing fast and the market was bursting at the seams. Each day merged into the next, and the control Maxine and David exerted encouraged employees to follow their lead, rather than be proactive. She wanted to articulate a culture that changed that. Gathering employees together, she explained what she wanted. How could you ensure there was a consistency between how someone at a store on the Gold Coast and one in Victoria would act? How did they view the culture of the business they turned up to each morning? In her head, she wanted it to be casual and fun. But it needed to be respectful too. It had to reflect the market and the product. The new CARE program, which outlined a system of customer care, was working, but it didn't deal with team members and how they should act.

John Weir knew that the 'fish philosophy', as it is termed across the globe, would perfectly fit their workplace culture. 'I went and bought the books and I was consuming one of them every flight I was on,' he says now. Read any of the books, articles, or business tips that come from the fish philosophy and you'll see that it revolves around four central tenets: choosing one's attitude; playing at work; making someone's day; and being present. 'They are simple sentences that you can use,' Weir says. And while the similarities between fish and mobile phones were limited, the idea sat perfectly with Maxine, and like disparate businesses around the world, it quickly became the foundation for the culture inside Vita Group.

'Then we said okay, now we want to come up with a name for it that's ours and we came up with VIBE,'

Maxine says – VIBE stands for Vibrant Innovative Business Environment. All of those elements fitted neatly with Maxine's view of the culture she wanted, and it remains today, although in different forms. Now, the company talks about the Vita VIBE as a way of doing business. Its internal magazine even bears the name VIBE. Recruits need the Vita VIBE. Salespeople do better with the Vita VIBE. Meetings are more innovative if attendees present the Vita VIBE.

'We try to bring it to life and make it a tangible thing,' Maxine says. That's not as easy as it sounds. A culture is the practical embodiment of the company's values. But how do you explain a vibe? And how do you know if a new recruit has it? Maxine says it stands out to her; it's the way people handle themselves, the way they can have fun, set aggressive goals and 'really go for them'. The company's culture also requires team members to be supportive in developing others. 'You're not just a passenger; you're there to learn and grow as part of the experience.'

Wayne Smith joined in 2006 and remembers culture being the topic of his first conversation with Maxine. He says she always used the explanation that if you looked after your people, they would then look after your customers, who would make you money. 'A lot of CEOs say that; a lot less do it in practice,' he says.

Maxine says culture is easy to establish at one site, but gets tricky over multiple sites. 'But fish rots from the head,' she warns, and as you get bigger, how do you know the culture on show at one store is the same that is on show at a further 40 or 80 or 100 stores? She says the company structure helps. Each store has a business manager. Each set of six to eight stores then has an area manager. Area managers feed into regional managers and then the leadership team.

'A culture has to be set out and explained. It's no use being in my head. It needs to be public and it needs a program to hold it together. You can't let a culture just grow organically. It can't just happen. You've got to make it happen and you have to enact it every single day and the way you do that is through your leaders. And that's why we really focus on our leaders, and I use the term "the shadow of a leader" constantly. The first thing that you should do if a business is not performing is go out and sit in front of it and watch it and feel it. You get the vibe of what is going on and nine times out of 10, it's because the leader is not doing his or her job.'

Vita Group's culture is unashamedly performance-driven. Its team members like to win, like their CEO.

'Even though we are now running Telstra stores, you hear a lot of conversations around the office about us winning, being better than other stores,' Maxine says. 'I think we kick them out of the park. So we are performance-driven, and competitive. But you can still have fun too.'

That means 'onesie days' in the office, where Maxine will arrive, dressed casually like everyone else, or gala dinners which are always fancy dress, or store employees dressing up in red to celebrate Valentine's Day. Ideas are encouraged and workshopped at a store level. But one strong rule applies: it must not be disrespectful.

'It is about having a bit of fun and laughing,' Maxine says. 'We take our work very seriously, but we don't take ourselves seriously.' That's obvious during the annual leaders' conference when Vita Group's 300 leaders get together to learn new skills, talk about business strategy, network and 'have a bit of fun'.

The support, coaching and training given to enhance the performance-driven nature of the company is crucial. To highlight that point, Maxine tells the story of one business manager who called before Christmas to explain that the sister of someone in his store had had their home burnt down. 'He asked me if we could provide some second-hand iPads for the kids. And of course we did. That shows he cared, and I like that. That's about culture. And when we talk about care here, it's not just about caring for the customer, it's caring about everything – about the way you look and the way you talk to people and the way you care for each of your team members.'

Dick Simpson puts it this way: 'It's about the way that the company will behave. It's about the interaction that you have with it as a customer or an employee. It's about the approach of people, the sorts of questions that they will ask you.' Simpson makes the point that companies have to be strong too; economic interests can test the culture of an organisation. 'For example, I met with Maxine recently and the first discussion we had was about the floods in Queensland and whether all the staff were okay. And she said they had closed those stores and let people go home. That's a personal value – it's not in our economic interest.' Like most boards, Vita Group directors regularly review the organisation's culture. 'And any decision that we make has to pass through the screen of "does it fit our culture?". And if it isn't culturally right, we'd find that.'

While culture is the enactment of the company's values, one drives the other, and Maxine says it was a mistake for the business to develop its VIBE culture before pinpointing its eight core values. If she had her time again, she'd do it the other way around.

'It wasn't that those values didn't exist, but I hadn't articulated them, and to be honest they've also grown over time,' she says. But once established, an organisation's culture also needs to be checked and frequently maintained, in the same way you have your car serviced at regular intervals.

Maxine found that out the hard way in November 2005 when her 'third child', the business she and David had nurtured from birth, floated on the public stock exchange. Perhaps, in retrospect, she should have seen that coming. Why else would she have been at the Melbourne Cup in the days before, just arriving at the Brisbane stock exchange to see her own little piece of history going public?

'It felt like a little bit of betrayal from my perspective,' she says. The float was very profitable personally – she and David took home $30 million. 'I believed I'd made it then and it changed things. It changed how I saw it, and I think it changed the culture.' Maxine and David's stake in Vita Group fell to 45 per cent on public listing. 'And when that happened, I thought, "What do I do now?" It was like everything that we had worked for had happened – and I lost my purpose.'

She felt under pressure to behave differently. All along, since the early 1990s, she had been focused on building a family business and creating a team. She saw it as her business and her team, and an enormous amount of emotional energy went into that. Then, all of a sudden, she felt the pressure to look, constantly, at the bottom line. 'Everyone made a big deal about you being publicly listed and I was thinking it must be different then, and I need to be different.'

Up until that point, Maxine had used a philosophy of 'look after your people first who in turn will look after your customers, who will love the environment that you have created and will keep coming back'. It was a trust cycle that had led to this point. But with the public listening, her focus changed.

'I was talking about how we were going to make more money and not what we were going to do,' she says. 'For the first time in my life, I didn't want to go to work, I had no desire to turn up on a Monday. And that had never happened to me before. I felt that I wasn't adding value any more. It took me a while to really understand that, and acknowledge it and try and work out why I was feeling that way.'

It took close to 18 months for Maxine to feel a real part of the business she'd given birth to back in 1993. 'I can't explain it other than saying I lost my way. I thought that I had made it and I went into no-man's land for about two years. Looking back, it was as though I didn't do anything during that time. Sure, I came to work. I turned up. But I wasn't contributing. I felt as though it all belonged to someone else.'

As is often the case, a crisis created a circuit breaker. The GFC loomed and Maxine had to throw herself back into the business. She took up, where in her mind, she let go.

'I'd devalued this business through not being a great leader – by thinking it's all done and it will run itself,' she says. 'Lesson learnt. No business will run itself.' It was that threat of losing everything that she had worked so hard for that prompted her into action. 'I don't know if you call it crisis management or just fear,' she says, 'but some people crave success while others fear failure. I fear failure.' Indeed, Maxine says that fear drives her success. 'I don't crave to be number one. I don't need everyone to say I'm fantastic, or successful. I just don't want anyone to see me as a failure. In reality, at the time of the GFC, that was what was driving me. I think that's what still hurts about my divorce; I feel as though I failed to provide my children with a family forever.'

In Maxine's Words

Q: What is the overriding prerequisite for a recruit to fit into your team?

A: Number one for me is the culture fit. They have to fit the business. I have brought people into this company that technically have been brilliant but they did not fit the culture so it did not work out.

Q: More specifically, when you consider someone, what are the big picture qualities you are looking for?

A: There are two main requirements to work here. First, you have to fit the culture and second, you need to be able to show respect. You cannot come into this company and bag previous people. You cannot come in and say, 'Why do you do this, this is crap, we do it much better over here'. You can't do that.

Straight away you will have people's backs up and they will not listen to you. So when I'm recruiting I pay attention to those two things.

Q: You haven't mentioned the recruit's expertise. How important is that?

A: As I've said I employ for will, not skill. But once I've established that the person would be a strong cultural fit, and that they would show the respect this business's history demands, I look to the technical skill set – whether that be financial, marketing, operational execution, project management, or something else.

Q: Do you mind what the person's personality is like? Do you look for something in particular?

A: I try to ascertain whether a recruit is an introvert or extrovert. You can't have a leadership team full of extroverts and you need a balance of both.

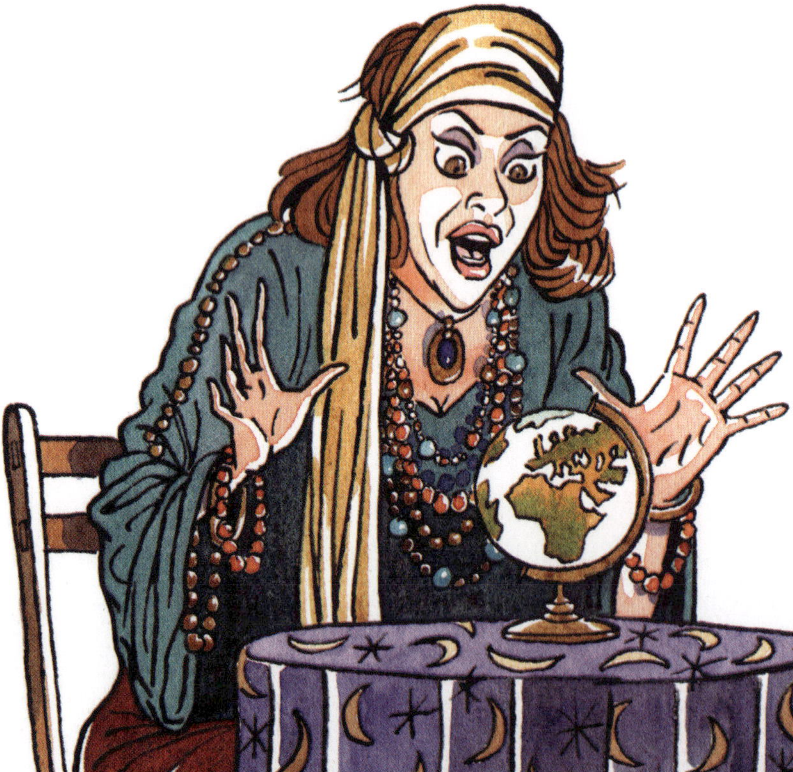

15.

Look Over the Fence

'Any fool can know. The point is to understand.' – Albert Einstein

One day in 1996, Maxine Horne needed a new vacuum cleaner. She headed for a well-known mass retailer, selected the model without too much fuss and opened her handbag to pay.

'Would you like an extended warranty?' the attendant asked.

'No, thanks,' Maxine replied. She turned on her heels and headed home with her new purchase.

The next day it was the offer of an extended warranty,

not the vacuum cleaner, that dominated her thoughts. Customers sought peace of mind when they bought a new phone, and this was an ideal way of providing it. Few ideas are original, and whether it's the arts, politics or business, ideas are adopted, modified and used in different ways in different circumstances. But it was that simple question – would you like an extended warranty – that prompted Maxine to re-examine what the business she and David owned was offering, and to act.

In 1996, she set up an ESP – extended service package – to mirror what had been offered to her a few weeks earlier. 'I walked away with absolute clarity thinking we needed to introduce an extended warranty – and I did.'

At the time, if something went wrong with your mobile phone, it was not possible to get a replacement on loan. That, in itself, could cause considerable inconvenience because it meant you could be without a phone for up to 12 weeks while it was sent to a repairer. Usually the retailer could not specify when a customer's phone would be ready for collection, or even what the problem might be; that was someone else's expertise. Each month the wait for repairs seemed to increase, because the industry was expanding exponentially, and manufacturers cared more about rolling out new handsets than fixing old ones. Service departments were poorly funded and backlogs were long. And to rub salt into the wound, contracts stipulated that you had to keep paying your monthly rental while your phone was being repaired! The inconvenience continued with a disconnect between the manufacturer's warranty and the terms of individual phone contracts. For example, the warranty could run for 12 months, but the contract was for 24 months.

'That meant if in month 13 something went wrong with your phone you weren't covered by the warranty,' Maxine says. With that context, she knew an extended warranty which included an allowance for every customer to receive a loan phone would work a treat at Fone Zone.

The extended service package turned out to be a hit and went on to deliver a healthy annual net profit. It was later ended with the adoption of a new warranty package after the Vita Group partnered with Telstra.

'The lesson here is pretty basic,' Maxine says. 'It's easy to become fixated with your own industry, but we shouldn't. It's important to look outside to ideas being tried or used. That's what happened with the extended service package. It came directly from another company's warranty offer. I saw it, knew it would work for us, and then adopted it.'

Implementing new products or processes requires confidence, especially when the views of others might differ from yours. Maxine had a gut feeling that an ESP would work in her industry, in the same way it worked on electrical goods. But not everyone shared her view, and its introduction was shaky. It was new to the industry and needed time to work. It's not unusual for new ideas to take time to latch on; customers are creatures of habit.

Lessons in business leadership from **Maxine Horne**

'When I first came up with ESP people told me I was nuts; that customers would never pay for it and I'd be lucky to sell 10 of them. So I became the product manager and every day I would get reports on how many handsets were sold and I would ring every store and say, "Tell me what happened yesterday – tell me about that sales conversation that you had where you didn't sell ESP, what was the difference with the one where you did?".' It took 18 months before the extended warranty package really took off, and it was tweaked along the way too. Originally, customers were offered a 12-month warranty, but it was then extended to 24 months, at a cost of $129.

'It's like your house insurance or car insurance or personal insurance,' Maxine says. 'People adopted it and really wanted to be covered – just in case.'

Maxine believes it would have taken off earlier if team members had seen greater value in it, but they didn't and struggled to convince customers. That was one of the reasons the package was amended.

'I needed to win over those selling it before customers would buy it so I needed to add more value,' she says. 'That's when we came back with a guaranteed replacement and a 10 per cent discount on your new handset when you traded it in.' Take-up surged and within four years, for every handset sold, 60 per cent of customers paid for an extended warranty. 'We would take people through the whole solution-selling, and we would spend time finding out about individual customers

– whether they were active and liked bushwalking, for example – and then we could tailor our discussion around that. It allowed us to grow our relationship with the customer.'

The vacuum cleaner story is taken from Maxine's everyday life which has proved time and again to be fertile ground for idea creation. A conversation about the mundane – in this case, the need to vacuum – earnt Vita Group a tidy profit. Often ideas present themselves like that and it's worthwhile reconsidering the start of the Fone Zone business. The initial concept to sell mobile phones through retail outlets in shopping centres – pioneered by Maxine and David – came from them seeing it happen elsewhere, and knowing, immediately, that it would work in Australia.

In mid-1994, the couple travelled to New Zealand and then back to the UK for a friend's wedding. A lot hadn't changed and the two years they had been living in Australia seemed like a short pause in a long sentence. But one change was immediately noticeable: mobile phones were everywhere. People were carrying them around in handbags, buying them at shopping centres, and using them for conversation. In Australia, that was not yet the case. They remained the domain of the business world, usually sold in out of the way places, and costing a small fortune. Maxine recalled the Carphone Warehouse boasting a number of stores when she left for Australia; but now they seemed to be located on every street corner. And those street corners were not just those lining industrial estates; they were encroaching on retail areas as part of a broad 'consumerisation' of mobile phones. The demographics of users were changing too; it had broadened beyond the reach of business. It seemed everyone wanted one.

'We were talking to friends in the industry and it had just moved on so much in such a short period of time,' Maxine says. 'Mobile phones had become a consumer item and the networks were driving that. They were all about getting as much market share as they could.'

This is the point where the entrepreneur often differs from the manager. Maxine witnessed what was happening in the UK and knew it was a business wave she could ride all the way back to Australia. She and David were prepared to work hard, and any venture involved some risk, but they knew the trend was coming. However, when they returned, they found that not everyone agreed. Indeed, shopping centre managers didn't like the idea at all. It wasn't a tradition customers liked, Maxine was told, before being shown a single piece of evidence.

'They said there were no mobile phone retailers in shopping centres – basically as proof that they wouldn't sell there,' she says.

This story is crucial to the success of Fone Zone, because Maxine and David's decision to press on and open their first retail store on the Gold Coast was the single decision that set them up for the next 20 years. It was a punt, because it hadn't been done before, and customers can sometimes show a reluctance to change their habits. But it worked elsewhere, and they believed it would work here.

In December 1994 they opened that first store as an Optus dealer. A month later, they had swapped to Telstra, and the store was branded Fone Zone. Its success was immediate and significant, and stores at Indooroopilly, the Myer Centre, and Toombul in Brisbane; Parramatta and Eastgardens in Sydney; and Southlands, Highpoint and Airport West in Melbourne quickly followed. Like the purchase of a vacuum cleaner, looking elsewhere had brought a great idea back home.

Maxine says the process of coming up with ideas fits better with an optimistic personality. 'I see opportunity when others might go straight to the negative and it really frustrates me,' she says. 'We had a person working for us who was always negative. One day I said to him, "You're the type of person who if you won lotto you'd probably worry about getting prank calls!". I am very optimistic and I'll always look for opportunities in everyday life.'

As the retail store idea showed, Australian businesses have the advantage of seeing what works – and what doesn't work – in the northern hemisphere before jumping through the same hoops here.

'My advice would be that firstly, particularly in today's world, is the need to really understand what business you are in. Once you have done that, you should look elsewhere in the world.' She says the big retailers follow the Tescos and Sainsburys in the UK the same way. 'That's just how it is. The first thing you need to do is a whole heap of research about what's going on globally. The next thing you do, once you've found where the industry is overseas, is to analyse how that might be relevant to the market here.' Maxine says that has been reinforced since the initial trip to her friend's wedding in the UK back in 1994. 'I was on a retail study tour with Westfield and we went right around the US and they lined up a whole series of meetings with chief financial officers and chief executive officers, and so on. We had this presentation from someone senior at Williams-Sonoma. She was talking to us about her strategy and basically it was to have a brand and chain of stores for every room that you have in the house. So they had a brand for kitchens, one for kids' bedrooms, and one for teenage girls. I asked her what percentage of the population were teenage girls and she said it was small, but didn't see a problem with that. I said, "I don't understand how you can build a brand on a small per cent of your population." She told me when you have 315 million people you can do anything. That's when my light bulb went on.'

Maxine realised that specific thinking wouldn't work in Australia because of our smaller population. Two per cent of 20 million is a limited captured audience. 'So it's good to look globally at what is going on, but you must keep that relevance to Australia,' she says. 'And relevance in Australia requires you to look at the size of population and the geography – just to name a couple of factors –

because it is harder to transport things from A to B here than it is elsewhere.'

After the global assessment and an analysis of its relevance to Australia, you look at your customers. What are they thinking? What are they talking about? Wanting? Doing? What are their aspirations? The next step in putting an idea into practice is to meet not only the needs of those customers, but their aspirations or wants. 'You have to look at their wants because, in the main, people don't need anything today,' Maxine says.

It would be remiss here not to mention Maxine's lack of modern technology know-how. She has worked in every part of her business, but that doesn't mean she's a tech-whiz. It was a matter of looking elsewhere, and studying the trends, not understanding the minutiae of the mobile phone being sold in the UK, that made her and David's decision to moved into retail stores a good one.

'The reality is I'm not a very technical person,' she admits. 'What I am good at is bringing people along on the journey.' If Maxine's computer breaks down, like many of us, she calls the IT department to fix it. 'My strength is seeing the opportunity and working out what this means, working through that, selling the vision and keeping people aligned to that vision.' It sounds very much like the description of a salesperson. 'Well, that's what I am. My job is to sell this business externally, and also to sell the vision to my people, and the strategy to my people. That means I need to explain to them why we are doing something and what their specific role in that might be.'

Vita Group has gone from a small family operation where Maxine and David made all the big decisions at the breakfast table with two toddlers underfoot to a national ASX-listed powerhouse. They've achieved this by keeping an eye on those doing business in their industry, as well as those in other industries. The company's approach is today more scientific and involves a huge amount of desktop research on sales data and customer segments. But that's not the reason to look past a good idea that pops up in conversation. Nowadays, the leadership team routinely examines different organisations — from how they market themselves to their corporate structures — and different industries, with a fresh set of eyes. Expert consultants bring their advice. Corporate executive studies are used. But in the end, a good idea can come from anywhere.

'There's one catch, though,' Maxine says. 'The idea has to match the company's values. Or it just doesn't work.'

In Maxine's Words

'Ideas often come from someone else; an experience I've had, or a reaction I've had. The extended warranty and the idea of selling from retail stores both came from experiences elsewhere. But I also get ideas at the oddest of times, and sometimes in the oddest of places. For example, I get a lot of ideas when I'm driving – in the same way others get them in the shower. I get behind the wheel of my car and start thinking of different places and things. But experience is the best basis for new ideas. If I have a good experience I'll think how could I mould that into my business. And if I have a bad experience, I think, how do I make sure that doesn't happen in my business.'

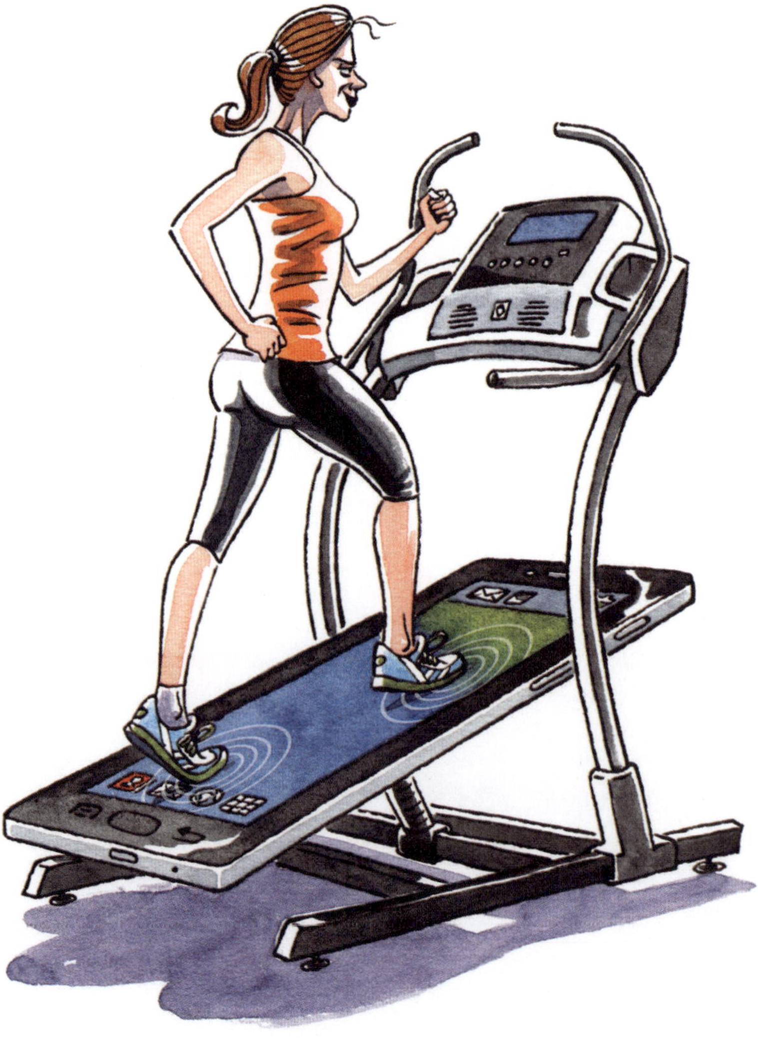

16.

Take Care of Yourself

'Take care of your body. It's the only place you have to live.'
– Jim Rohn, entrepreneur and author

For the past six years, each morning before dawn, Maxine Horne can be found at an inner-city Brisbane gym. Here, under the watchful eye of trainer Nathan Barrett, she runs hard. A weights program that focuses equally on her upper body and lower body is the mainstay of her routine, but it also includes conditioning and cardio, as well as boxing.

'Any changes that have occurred in Maxine's fitness are of her own making,' Barrett says. 'I just turn up and give her some direction.' He says fitness trainers often come across clients who are looking for a 'pseudo psychologist' to chat to. 'Maxine is not like that. The hardest competition for her in here is herself. She's more competitive with herself than with any other person. She's always been fit, even when she was heavier.'

Four years ago Maxine was considerably heavier than she is today. She was a busy mother, a CEO, often the family driver. She wanted to be everything for everyone and it wasn't working.

'I didn't feel good about myself. I was overweight. I wasn't necessarily happy and back in 2011, I decided that the next year – 2012 – was going to be about me. I remember sitting the whole family down and saying to them this year is going to be about me because the last 20-odd years have been about everybody else.'

Maxine's position is that of many women, and some men, who try to do it all. Work–family balance is a goal, never quite attained, and it's easy to feel that you're not achieving at either work or home.

'I was the mum, the wife, the leader, and everyone would come to me, and there was nothing left. I put on about a kilogram a year and just didn't do anything about it. My kids came first, then my husband and then the business and then all of a sudden, I was quite unhappy with myself.' It's hard for that not to then spill over into the workplace. 'It did. I think I was angry. I was certainly frustrated. I knew I could be better and that would come out in my behaviour. If I'm honest, I think I grew intolerant of things that just didn't go how I wanted them to.'

Having repeatedly learnt the importance of seeking expert help at work, she did the same at home and was provided with a medically assessed diet. Over the next six months, she lost 23 kilograms.

'It was habit forming,' she says. 'I was never an unhealthy eater; it came down to portion sizes.' Losing weight pulled an important trigger for Maxine. It provided a newfound confidence. It provided a personal focus. She increased her gym visits and cut down on the snacks at work. 'I'm a bit of an all or nothing person, so if I was going to eat ice cream, I'd eat a bucket of it. I decided I wouldn't, and I didn't.' She says she used the planning skills from work, and the scheduling skills she used to stay on top of her children's activities, to create a routine. 'I had a whole schedule written out about when I would go to the gym, what I would do there, when I would walk at night, when I would eat, and what I would eat. Everything.'

The plan's gone now; but the discipline has remained despite two significant hiccups. The first was back surgery in mid-2012 thanks to a series of collapsed discs.

'We were in the Maldives and got around on bikes,' she says. 'We cycled everywhere, but every time I got on the bike, my back would twinge.' People with bad backs know what a 'twinge' can mean. Maxine didn't. 'I just thought it was because I had been cycling so much and I might have pulled a muscle.' On a work trip to Sydney soon after she arrived home, she struggled to walk off the plane. 'I remember them asking me if I wanted a chair and I told them I'd be fine. But I was failing. I drove home – I really am an idiot sometimes – and then went straight to the hospital.'

She had surgery to address bulges in lumbar spine discs L2, L3 and L4, which were impacting on her nerves. 'It set me back a bit but I'm very goal-oriented so within two to three months I was back training with Nathan. I was that determined. The physio told me I was the poster child for back surgery – but it was really important to me to get back on my feet.'

That was the first hurdle in Maxine's pursuit of fitness. But the close of 2012 brought a bigger challenge. Maxine split with her husband David, who left the company and remarried.

'I was devastated,' she says. 'I was emotional, not sleeping.' Often, she'd call her stepmother Susan. 'I would turn up at her home at 2 am and sit there bawling because I didn't want to break down in front of the kids. I felt like a zombie.' Sensibly, Maxine also visited her doctor. 'She told me she could see how upset I was but she advised me to keep eating well, exercising and sleeping. I remember her saying that everything would sort itself out. And that's what I did.'

Maxine had been with David for more than half her life and it left a gaping hole. They had built a business together, devising strategy at home, and planning new ventures on the way to work. And then, it was over.

Maxine tried to stay focused. 'I kept going to the gym; I'd haul my sorry arse there each morning,' she says. 'I wasn't feeling physically 100 per cent but I was doing it.'

It's not unusual that someone, faced with a crisis, takes the same steps each day. Routine helps. One foot in front of the other. But on one particular day in the gym, before most people were awake, it all became too much.

'I wasn't feeling great but I was doing it,' she says. 'I was in the gym and I did this exercise where you slam the ball onto the floor. I thought it was one of those that would absorb it. It wasn't. The ball had a big bounce in it, and it came straight back up and hit me in the face. It cut my lip, and that was the last straw.' She lay on the gym floor, crying. Her trainer knew something was amiss. He suggested they train elsewhere for a while. 'But I had to get over it. The next person who asked me where David was got an answer. I told them we had separated, and once it was out, it was much easier.'

The 'corporate athlete' tag for executives, explained by Jim Loehr and Tony Schwartz of the *Harvard Business Review* in 2001, highlights how physical capabilities form a foundation stone to sustained high performance. It's hard to find anyone who now disagrees, and for Maxine, it makes perfect sense. If you are fit, you feel better. Your mood is elevated. You sound and act sharper. You are able to work harder, and longer and smarter.

'Sleep matters,' she says. 'So does what you eat. And exercise is huge part of that. I feel different on the days that I don't exercise. It comes down to looking after yourself.' A commitment to those things, as part of her work day, also provides a new work–home balance, of sorts.

Maxine knows she is in a privileged position. She is able to employ a cleaner, book a weekend away without worrying too much about the cost, and could afford long day care when her children were small.

'I feel very grateful for all that; I know there are many women who are not able to do that, but I work very hard to make sure my team has that work–life balance.' She sets an example, leaving the office now at 5 pm. 'I want my children to know I care – that's why I do silly things like pack a school lunch for my 17-year-old daughter!' Guilt, as most working parents will acknowledge, plays a big role too. 'We ask a lot of our employees and I think for me it's just that law of reciprocation,' she says. 'Why should I care whether someone worked 9 am until 5 pm or even 9 am until 3 pm, went and did something with their children, and then did another two hours work at night? It's about being flexible and not making people feel guilty about putting their family first – because they should. You will often hear me say, "Go. The business won't collapse because you aren't here. But your kid will remember that they had to wait for hours for you."'

MAXINE'S DAY

Maxine starts her day at 4.30 am and goes to bed by 9 pm if she's not going out. She lost 23 kilograms in just over six months on a medical diet that focused on healthy food without carbohydrates.

Breakfast: a cup of tea and scrambled eggs
Morning tea: a protein bar at work. If at home, she'd have fruit with a spoonful of yoghurt
Lunch: a tuna salad
Afternoon tea: this would mirror morning tea
Dinner: meat and vegetables

Maxine drinks four litres of water each day and never drinks wine at home by herself. 'I'll have a drink when I go out but for me to lose weight I can't drink any alcohol or coffee. I've learnt about portion size more than content. I've always eaten fairly well, but I've reduced the portion size.'

Managing your energy to perform (lead) better – Rupert Bryce, Executive Coach, Performing Strategies

1. The biggest drain on energy is when you don't value or enjoy your work. Aligning your goals, personal values and the type of work you do creates sustainable energy. Awareness of what is important to us is the source of all energy and motivation.

2. The second biggest drain on energy is lack of sleep – most leaders don't understand how a lack of sleep will kill productivity, memory, concentration and increase negative emotions. Most (97.5 per cent) people need at least seven hours sleep to be their best but half of my clients fail to consider the known facts about sleep. Why? It becomes a behaviour that is hard to break and the impact is usually on their staff and families.

3. The third biggest drain on energy is nutrition. Diets low in antioxidants and essential nutrients have consistently been shown to cause and contribute to illness and disease. A poor diet combined with stress and fatigue can be very damaging to your health, let alone your performance at work. Listening to your body and eating whole foods are easy choices with a large impact on work productivity.

4. Making connections, finding meaning, and solving problems are executive tasks that require lightning-fast electrical impulses between areas of the brain. Leaders are primarily paid to synthesise and filter complex data – any behavioural choices that detract from that ability are self-defeating. The most common of the self-defeating behaviours is drinking more than two standard drinks of alcohol.

5. According to many studies, people who exercise are more productive and happier. Workers who engage in regular physical activity perform better – both in terms of quality and quantity of work – so why don't we exercise as much as we should? Usually it is because of one or more of the issues outlined above.

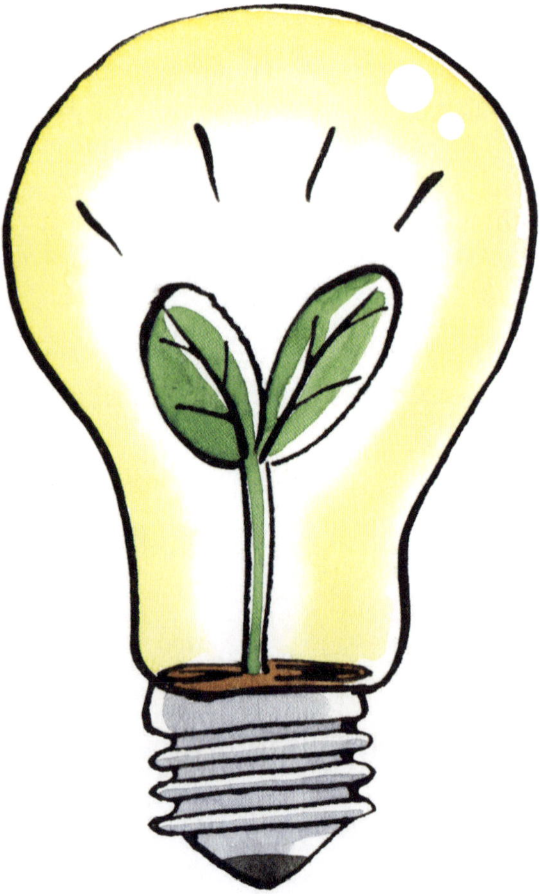

17.

Think Smart

'A business has to be involving, it has to be fun and it has to exercise your creative instincts.' – Richard Branson, founder and executive chairman of Virgin Industries

Seinfeld, the popular NBC television sitcom that ran for nine years, is pretty much about nothing: a phone message, a note, a baby shower, a library. The genius lies in the comedic turn the actors put on those everyday moments we all experience. Often, the best business ideas have similar roots. A moment in time: standing in the shower; frustration at waiting in a long queue; poring over your child's homework; or even an inability to make something work the way you want. Everyday life serves up countless moments that entrepreneurs use as the impetus for ideas that sometimes become rivers of gold. Modern technology helps too, offering cheap marketing and distribution channels and crowdfunding for those needing money. But the impetus for any of that has to be the idea; the little seed that with planning and the right infrastructure can blossom and line the pockets of those who dare to dream.

When Maxine and David arrived in Australia in May 1992, they rented a bungalow-type home in the Brisbane suburb of Chapel Hill. Coming from the UK, the house only needed one attribute to make them happy: a swimming pool. So they paid the rent, moved in without much furniture – a two-seater sofa, a green plastic garden table with chair, a bed and a TV – and spent most of their free time around the pool, marvelling at the life on offer in Australia and how markedly it differed from the UK's cold climes. A few weeks after arriving, Maxine started work with Optus Mobile Communications as an account manager on an annual income of $51,000. Two months later, David got a job as a sales representative with Exicom.

Not long after starting work, Maxine met and befriended James Bellas, and one afternoon, while on a work road trip, they began discussing why the dealers' focus was on selling handsets when they could be making more money selling the network. They wondered what would stop someone establishing a dealership which would connect mobile phone users to the Optus network. They mulled it over, threw some more ideas around, and went home.

Teachers will tell you that individual students learn differently. Some are visual learners; others learn by speaking out loud. Others need to write information down, to draw the dots, and link them. Maxine still has a habit of drawing pictures, columns, key notes; skills she has used since her school days in Wales. One Friday night, soon after that work trip with James Bellas, she sat half-listening to the television. David, on the two-seater, was engrossed. With a pad and pen in hand, Maxine began plotting something, trying to make the figures in her head come alive on paper.

'I was thinking that if you did X amount of connections and you got X amount of payment for those connections, what that would mean,' she says. She was colouring in the idea she and James had talked about; the idea of selling the network, not the handset. She spent a few hours drawing up columns, formulating a rudimentary financial statement where expenses were low and turnover high, and where the potential for an annuity stream existed. She did it again the next night, and the next, and started to think it was an idea that could take their dreams beyond the Chapel Hill renter with the backyard pool.

The 29 year old knew they would have to be brave to make it work. 'I was on the cusp of something and I thought we needed to give it a real go. We'd already uprooted our lives, moved to another country, and sold nearly everything we had. If it didn't work, what's the worst thing that would happen? We'd just go and find ourselves another job.' Her expectations weren't high. She didn't see herself as heading a multi-million dollar company with thousands of employees. She didn't see herself or her husband on Australia's rich lists, or pounding the boardroom table negotiating deals. Back then, she was a new wife, with a plan to work, save money, and enjoy the fabulous Australian lifestyle. She and David also dreamt of owning their own Brisbane home; one with a flash pool that they could sit around with friends on the weekend.

The business plan Maxine was nutting out was entirely different to what the rest of the market was doing. She could see how much more profitable selling the network would be and she knew it wouldn't require a pot of cash to start up. It was no more than the idea she and James had chatted about, and she couldn't see why it wouldn't succeed. At work, she and James discussed the idea some more, and a few months later they did something about it. Maxine and David joined James and his partner Julie to start a business called Queensland Network Options, QNO. Each couple outlaid $2000. Twelve months after landing in Australia, in May 1993, the couples employed three salespeople and opened for business out of a tiny office in Stones Corner in Brisbane. The aim was to make it easy for customers, and make money in the process. To that end, customers would keep the same phone and the same number, which most found appealing. Then, under the deal offered by QNO, they would get connected for 20 per cent less than they would have otherwise.

'One of the reasons small businesses go under is that they invest too much in their stock, and they haven't got enough cash flow, but this business didn't need that so for me it was quite logical,' Maxine says.

QNO was a sideline at first. Maxine and James kept their jobs at Optus Mobile Communications and David remained at Exicom. James' partner Julie ran the QNO business. It was hard work, and frequently they would start at 5 am and continue until after midnight. At the four-month mark, more funds were needed to allow QNO to keep trading, and at that point James and Julie opted out. Maxine says she used $20,000 from the sale of her house in Birmingham to keep QNO trading. The long hours continued. The backyard pool in their Chapel Hill renter was used less and less.

Something had to give and in January 1994, David quit his job at Exicom to work on QNO full time. Maxine says the couple lived off her income. Suppliers and creditors needed to be paid, staff dealt with, and tax paid. Connections onto the Optus network had to be processed. Weekends disappeared under a mountain of paper. But the business was working. Money was walking through the door. The idea, plotted out with a pen and paper 18 months earlier, was growing and it wasn't much longer before Maxine quit her job to work full time on QNO. They were both drawing $24,000 each year.

Over time their sales team increased, with Maxine and David targeting people who sold Amway health, beauty and homecare products. That was a clever idea, as anyone who has been on the receiving end of an Amway sales pitch would know. Amway sellers stood out as confident and determined. They wanted the sale more than anything. The business trajectory for QNO, which then morphed into Australian Network Options (ANO), continued to skyrocket, proof the idea plotted out by Maxine and James was good, and the sales team, which also grew quickly, stood out to peer businesses.

At one point, Maxine remembers, Optus held ANO up as an example to other dealers, divulging that it had achieved more than 4000 connections the previous month. That meant Maxine and David's staff had given Optus more than 4000 new customers. Their closest competitor had scored 'around 80'.

'The whole room turned and looked at us and I remember distinctly saying to David that this was going to spell trouble. And from that day, it did. Our sales team was headhunted and offered a lot more money.' They lost some of their best people in following weeks, who were lured away by extravagant commissions. More dealers opened quickly too, capitalising on the pot of gold that QNO and then ANO seemed to monopolise. Both these factors stymied growth.

Good ideas are not always good long term. Timing

is crucial. Take the first mobile phone for example; a great idea but it has changed umpteen times over the years, and convergence means that will continue. Now, with increased competition and the need to pay higher commissions, Maxine and David knew there had to be another model that they could capitalise on.

In mid-1994, Maxine and David went for a holiday, first to New Zealand and then back to UK for a friend's wedding. They immediately noticed the massive proliferation of mobile phones which were no longer just high-end business tools. They were everywhere and could be bought everywhere too. This is a crucial point, because ideas grow and change. A new idea can be an old one, tweaked. Or it might mean a change in demographics or sales geography or price point. The same idea, with a twist. In the UK, as is covered in another lesson in this book, mobile phones were no longer sold in business or industrial estates. In the time Maxine and David had been in Australia, mobile phones had become a High Street purchase.

'It became really clear to me,' Maxine says, 'that you had to be in a shopping centre if you were going to sell a consumer product.' Bingo. They had their next business strategy – they would move from only selling the network to become a fully-fledged retail business, in a retail environment.

Being an Optus dealer, that was their first point of call. However, Maxine says Optus didn't agree with the shopping centre location for mobile phone sales.

With their exclusive Optus dealership, that made their initiative difficult. They had a plan and a strategy, but Optus didn't want to get on board. A reluctance also surfaced among shopping centre lease managers who didn't think mobile phones would sell.

'I remember having this discussion with a shopping centre manager who told me people don't buy phones from shopping centres. I said that's because they can't!' With Optus not interested, Maxine and David decided to go and pitch it to Vodafone and Telstra. Vodafone was uninterested but Telstra was. 'They were all over us. At the time we thought that was because they believed we were are pair of geniuses. Later, we realised it wasn't.' Telstra knew QNO was taking up to 4000 connections off them each month. 'Even if we swapped from Optus to Telstra and didn't do anything else, we still brought with us up to 4000 connections a month.' That was gold for the big telco and not long after QNO – which by then had become Fone Zone – signed an exclusive deal with Telstra. It would continue trading under the Fone Zone brand, but that one idea, tweaked and adapted over time, formed the beginning of a fruitful partnership that continues to this day.

The idea to sell the network and then to become a retail outlet had worked a treat. It was a substantial idea that a business could grow around. Of course, ideas don't have to be that big, or even that sustainable. They can be short and sweet, or add to one part of the business, or be used across the business in different ways. The important element is to be prepared to change focus and adapt. Modern history is littered with examples of companies that didn't see the next wave of technology or the next economic tsunami forming offshore. Vita Group would not be enjoying its current position in the market if it had remained a family business, or if it was not floated, or if it did not look, constantly, at what might be the next threat, or the next opportunity. Ideas can envelop both.

Maxine cites the decisions to welcome private equity into the company in 2002, and three years later to publicly list as critical. Both ideas grew out of the need to change. Fone Zone was growing quickly in the lead-up to 2002, and other brands were joining the market too. In 1998, according to ABN-AMRO, less than 30 per cent of the Australian population had mobile phones; by 2002, that figure had increased to 65 per cent. In the five years to 2003, prepaid customers increased by 36 per cent. The growth made multi-millionaires of many, says Neville Threader, who has worked with Telstra, and Maxine, for more than 20 years. 'You would open the front door of any Telstra dealership and a truck would back up and let money in. The business was so busy and such a growth industry.'

But it was that growth that prompted Fone Zone to look at what would happen next, and the idea turned to acquisition.

'It couldn't grow at that rate forever,' Maxine says, 'so we had to change strategy and embark on a path of acquisition.' For that to occur, they needed capital, and it was out of that need that an injection of private equity ensued. This, three years later, led to the public float. But a few years after that, in 2009, another idea was needed to ensure growth continued. That's when the idea of a master licence with Telstra surfaced. This had not existed before and it took the partnership from one where Fone Zone acted as a Telstra dealer to one where it would be granted up to 100 Telstra stores to run.

Sprout Accessories, a new arm that offers consumers everything from chargers to mobile phone covers, is an addition to the business which meets the demands of the market that sees mobile phones as fashion.

'Before we started Sprout we used to buy accessories from distributors and then we would sell them on,' Maxine says. 'It's high volume, high margin. As a result we have a very successful business in its own right, run by a small niche team.'

Generating new ideas is open to all team members, and they take it up. Maxine gives the example of Luke Wadeson who worked with Telstra and a third party software support provider to supply computer tablets for Queensland police officers.

That innovation focus is also the direction the Vita Group wants to follow with small-to-medium businesses, as well as retail stores, and it reflects the changing use of mobile phones. Once, they served as a business tool, purely for simple communication. Along the way, they became part of families' lives, offering an ability to stay in touch and to improve security. They've morphed from a discretionary buy in our private lives to a compulsory one. We use them to take photographs, get fit and study a foreign language. Concurrently, their use in business has exploded, allowing access to the internet, the ability to document meetings or notes, and expedite decisions. Rarely now is the mobile phone a simple means of communication.

'I honestly don't remember the last real conversation I had on the phone,' Maxine says, 'but I text and email constantly.'

The next step in how the mobile phone is used sets the direction for the ideas being worked up at Vita Group's Brisbane support centre. At a retail level, it targets the 'Internet of Things', which allows data to be transferred over a network without human involvement.

'They really should call it the Connectivity of Things,' Maxine says, 'because items like your fridge will have a sim card that will alert you on your way home from work that you need to stop and buy milk.' The ability for your fridge to dictate orders is already here, but manufacturers are still pondering the price point at which the mass market will pick it up. It's not just your fridge that will be programmed to be bossy. Your mobile phone will be able to act as your credit card, your air-conditioning unit will be able to judge your preferred temperature and set it so that it is reached as you walk through the front door. 'That means our ideas, for the retail market, have to come out of the connected home; an audit of what people want and how that is set up and then serviced.'

In the business space, work is further down the track, partly because of the convergence of the cloud. The demand there is for a service that helps business use the cloud.

'For example, if you're a small business that employs 20 plumbers, plumbing and not administration is going to be your expertise,' says Maxine. 'We go into a business, look at their desired outcome, what applications would be useful, integrate the infrastructure, install wifi points around that and then provide them with a service maintenance agreement.' This draws on the logic that provoked Fone Zone to switch its focus to the service, not just the handsets, it could offer retail customers. 'It's in our DNA to use the device as the conduit to sell other products and services. Our habit now is to think smart.'

In Maxine's Words

'When I walk around Vita Group's Brisbane support centre and hear the words "because we've always done it that way", it drives me insane. What it tells me is that we are not thinking about what we are doing, we are just doing it because someone has told us to. We are not challenging the status quo; we are not even wondering whether there is a better way to do things.'

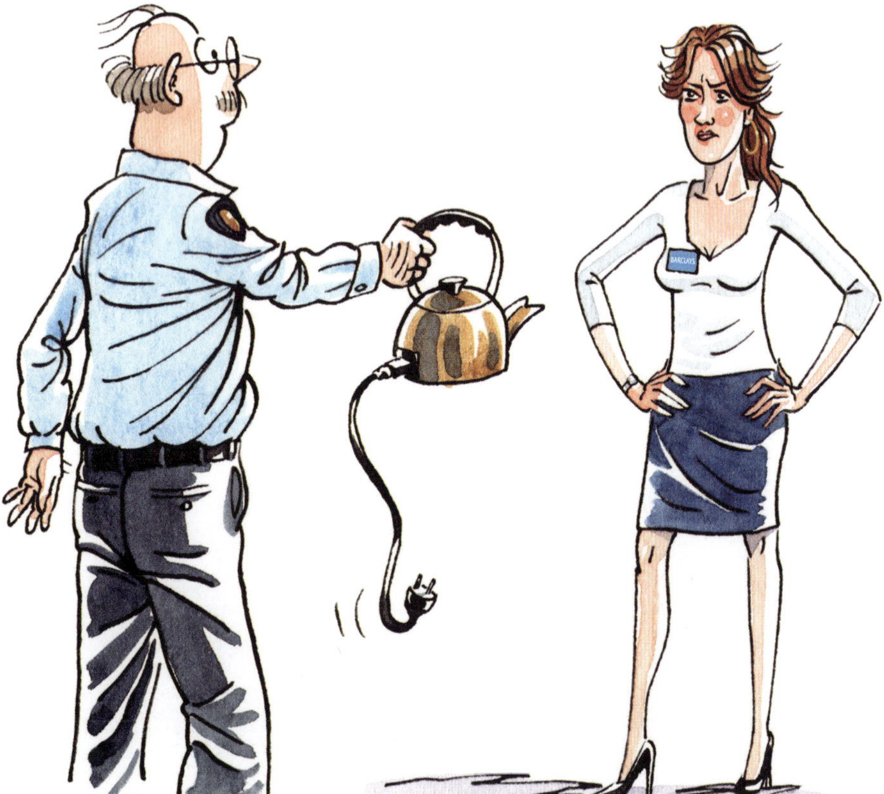

18.

Run Hard

'Winning is not a sometime thing; it's an all time thing. You don't win once in a while, you don't do things right once in a while, you do them right all the time. Winning is a habit. Unfortunately, so is losing.' – Vince Lombardi, NFL coach and winner of two Superbowls

It was over a pint one weekend at the local Caerphilly sports club that Maxine was challenged to a race in the local half-marathon being staged a couple of weeks hence. Now, more than three decades later, Maxine can't remember the name of the challenger, only that he was 'built like a brick shithouse'. He played rugby. She played netball. Both teams would gravitate to the bar on a Saturday afternoon. On this afternoon, he was showing off to his mates and anyone else who would listen.

'He'd had a few pints and told me – so everyone could hear – that he could beat me,' Maxine says. 'I looked at him and was sure he couldn't beat me over 500 metres, let alone a half-marathon.' So there, in front of all their friends, they put a 20-quid wager on it. Did she win? 'Of course I did – by about 20 minutes – and he had to pay up! I made sure it was on a Saturday night in front of everybody,' she adds with a laugh.

The contest had given her the taste to chase something bigger and, after winning that half-marathon, Maxine went on to train for the full London marathon. She still works in much the same way. Bigger and better. From the moment she was challenged, there wasn't any suggestion in her mind that she could lose.

'Don't ever say to me I can't do something,' she says. 'Because I'll just find a way to do it.' Maxine still feels she needs to prove herself; to her team, to her clients, to her investors, to her board. 'I honestly don't know where it comes from.' But she knows her success is largely driven by a challenge put out, or one accepted. 'I say to people now there is always a way; you just need to find it and make sacrifices to get there.'

It's not only the challenge that appeals, it's the contest that comes with it. As a student, Maxine would run home for a jam sandwich each day because she didn't want her classmates knowing her family circumstances meant she was entitled to lunch vouchers. The constant training improved her fitness. Then, one afternoon in track and field she decided to take on the top track performer, a fellow student from a wealthy family. She's not sure what prompted it; she just decided to give herself the challenge. She was going to win. But that wasn't the focus; the focus was on beating the school track star.

'I remember thinking, this is a challenge. I'm going to run and I'm going to beat her. I was challenging myself.' The race started. Maxine focused on the finishing line and didn't, for a moment, countenance that she might lose. 'I remember beating her by about a lap [over five miles]. The PE teacher come over and asked me my name. I told her and she asked me where my running shoes were. I said I didn't have any and she told me to follow her. We went over to lost property, she gave me a pair, and welcomed me to the track team.' Four decades on, Maxine remembers that conversation, verbatim. She could feel her self-confidence grow. She could run well and someone noticed it. She'd tasted victory and there wasn't anything sour about it.

Maxine's first job after completing high school was at Barclays Bank in the small Welsh village of Bargoed. Each morning, she'd make the 40-minute bus trip from the home she shared with her father, stepmother, sister and half-brothers. It developed a monotonous regularity. Her day consisted of filling out bank statements, putting them in envelopes, licking them and putting them through a stamp machine. She had another job, as all new interns did: she was required to make tea and coffee for the 50 members of staff three times a day. The first round was at 9.30 am, then 11 am, and then 3.30 pm. She did it with enthusiasm on day one, but by week's end, she thought it a waste of her time. Why did she have to do it? Wouldn't it be better to have a roster system? She said nothing, until a few days later, she was buzzed by the officer working on the security desk. It was 11 am.

'Where's my coffee?' he asked.

'My biggest claim to fame was that one day I created a riot,' Maxine says now. 'It was a silly tradition and I challenged it. I told him that I wouldn't be making it that day. It was a waste of my time and there should be a roster.'

This was a small branch of Barclays Bank where the supervisor had earnt his stripes over decades. New recruits were not meant to rock the boat. Already, Maxine's entry – on a management training program where recruits spent three months in different parts of the Barclays business – had raised eyebrows. And the audacity of the new recruit, without earning any stripes, to challenge their way of doing things only fed the long timers' scepticism about the program. But Maxine had announced she wasn't making coffee, and had no plans to back down. The day passed slowly and at day's end, she was told she needed to see the bank's manager.

'I said I wasn't doing it. I didn't mind doing my share but didn't think it was my job all day every day.' He didn't like it; she stood her ground. After two weeks, a roster was posted where all staff took turns to make the tea and coffee. The decision was not without short-term pain, though. 'The younger ones loved it and the older ones hated it and got me back big time by making me do all these shitty jobs like archiving.'

More than three decades on and Maxine is in the big office. How would she react now if a 19-year-old new recruit challenged the roster system?

'I'd say okay. I'd think good on them for believing what they do and speaking up about it. I like that.'

Rising to a challenge, or being driven by the competition it musters, is at the heart of both Maxine's personality and her business acumen. 'Challenging the status quo is in my DNA,' she says. 'When someone says why, I say why not.' It was one of the reasons that Tricia Mittens, one of Maxine's first employers, selected her from a pool of workers who were going to be fired. Tricia wanted to make up her own mind about whether Maxine deserved to stay.

'The reason it wasn't working before was because no-one was giving Maxine the direction she needed,' Tricia says now.

Maxine would accept any challenge and genuinely believed, through sheer determination, that she'd succeed. The stand out example to Tricia was Maxine's decision to re-plumb her own house. Maxine was in her early twenties and had never had any sort of training as a plumber. One Friday, she announced to the office that she was spending the weekend re-plumbing her small home. Maxine remembers the conversation. Her father was a plumber and she had seen him do odd jobs and couldn't countenance, for a moment, that she couldn't do what her father did.

'Instead of saying, like most people, that it was something she couldn't do, she said, "Who says I can't do that?" – and then set about doing it,' Tricia says. It should be noted that having the will to do something is significantly different to having the skill to do it and Maxine was forced, a week later, to employ an expert to finish the work she'd begun!

Tricia says whatever the strengths and weaknesses of an employee, the role played by their boss is crucial. 'If someone doesn't make it, before it's their fault, it's your fault. Invest the time and you get it back.' It's a belief Maxine has adopted with her own team.

The other factor in the challenges Maxine has taken on is discipline. To win a race, or run a half-marathon, you have to throw everything you have at it. In the same vein, to achieve strong profits, you have to be competitive. Running provided Maxine with a talent that allowed her, once she beat the track star, to get noticed. But discipline was just as important as talent.

'I'm not disciplined when it comes to something I don't value – but if it's something important to me, I put in 100 per cent,' she says. And there's nothing better to focus that discipline than a challenge. Over the years, it's been the raison d'être behind the company's success.

Maxine Horne doesn't fit the corporate mould. She is

savvy and outspoken and likes things done her way. She hasn't spent much time ingratiating herself into business networks or the millionaires' club. She runs her own race with one eye on the life she was born into and another on where she's headed. That means a business start-up was a perfect fit, and it was the decision by Maxine and David to question the status quo that prompted their first retail foray. If they had not challenged the prevailing view that mobile phones didn't sell in shopping centres, their company would not have had the lift-off it did. Nor perhaps would it today boast 1700 team members and an annual turnover of more than $600 million.

'It's not everyone's cup of tea, but I really enjoyed the challenge of getting the business up against the odds,' she says. 'I loved the camaraderie, the culture, and the idea that anything was possible. People too often say that you can't do anything because of the rules and I think, why not? I mean, what's going to happen? We're not breaking the law; we're just thinking in a different way. If we don't challenge things, we'll get the same that we've always got.'

Dick Simpson, Vita Group board chair, says his CEO will also readily accept a challenge issued to her by the board. 'If you challenge her, she might push back but then she always thinks about it. Often she'll come back a couple of days later and say that she had thought about it and how worthwhile the idea might be.'

Of course, you can suffer from 'challenge overdose', something Maxine is quick to explain to young entrepreneurs. 'It won't be successful every single time,' she says. 'You've got to be prepared for that. But all you need is for it to be successful once. Just once. You should continually challenge how things are done, or how you operate. If people didn't challenge things we wouldn't have an internet. There wouldn't be Google or Facebook.'

It's a hugely exciting time to be in the telco industry. The pace of data connections continues to increase in line with a phenomenon known as Moore's Law which says that the speed and memory capacity of a computer will double every two years (as it has done since the mid-1960s). Almost everyone carries a mobile device vastly more powerful than the technology we used to put man on the moon less than 50 years ago. People are more connected than ever and new functional uses keep arising for the handheld devices that are the core of Maxine's business. The sky is the limit but her strategy is based on the pillars it has forged from day one.

'We survived, at various times, because we put our people first, because we resisted volume and because we focused on service. All of that afforded us the ability to charge more,' she says. 'It's in our DNA to value-add; to see the core device as a conduit for selling everything else. That's why we are thinking smart and running hard.'

Chronology

- January 1993 – Queensland Network Options (QNO) starts with $2000 per couple
- April 1993 – James and Julie Bellas leave QNO
- September 1993 – Queensland Network Options (QNO) changes to Australian Network Options (ANO)
- September 1993 – Gaincroft registers and later becomes Fone Zone Pty Ltd
- November 1994 – ANO store at Pacific Fair opens as an Optus dealer
- January 1995 – Fone Zone establishes as a Telstra dealer
- January 1995 – First store at Pacific Fair rebrands as Fone Zone
- 1996 – Fone Zone 'sold' to Interact, but is stopped at the last minute and ends in court

- July 1996 – CARE launches
- October 1996 – ESP extended warranty program launches
- July 1998 – VIBE internal culture program launches
- January 2000 – Fone Zone signs Telstra Dealer Agreement for a further 5 years
- July 2000 – Fone Zone acquires The Mobile Phone Shop
- 2001 – Fone Zone wins Achievement Award for Retail Excellence (Australian Mobile Telecommunications Association)
- November 2001 – Fone Zone acquires Gould Holdings
- 2002 – Fone Zone wins Telstra National Dealer of the Year award (Solution Innovator)
- November 2002 – Investec Wentworth invests in Fone Zone
- 2003 – Fone Zone wins National Retailer of the Year (NRA) award
- 2003 – Fone Zone wins Telstra Excellence in Customer Service award
- 2003 – Fone Zone wins Best Mobile Phone Retailer award (*Australian Telecom Magazine* Awards)
- 2003 – Fone Zone wins Queensland Medium Business of the Year award (Australian Service Excellence awards)
- March 2003 – Fone Zone acquires Let's Talk Communications
- March 2003 – Fone Zone acquires In Touch Communications

- June 2003 – Fone Zone acquires MPC Communications
- July 2003 – Fone Zone acquires Call Direct
- November 2003 – Fone Zone acquires Phone Shack
- 2004 – Maxine Horne wins Right Management Consultants Award (Australian HR Awards)
- 2004 – Fone Zone wins Telstra BigPond Broadband Dealer of the Year Award (Australian Retail Association NSW)
- March 2004 – Fone Zone opens 100th store at Hornsby NSW
- 2005 – Fone Zone is certified by Customer Service Institute of Australia
- 2005 – Fone Zone wins Supreme Retailer of the Year; Innovation in Retail and Training; Human Resources Initiative Awards (National Retail Awards)
- March 2005 – Fone Zone acquires One Zero Communications
- July 2005 – Fone Zone signs Telstra Dealer Agreement for a further 5 years
- November 2005 – Fone Zone is publicly listed on the ASX at $1.00 per share
- 2006 – Fone Zone acquires Communique
- June 2006 – Fone Zone shares perform well, at $1.30
- October 2006 – Telstra Next G network launches
- June 2007 – Fone Zone shares dip to $0.68
- November 2007 – Fone Zone acquires Next Byte

- 2007/08 – Global financial crisis (GFC) hits
- April 2008 – Fone Zone shares hit by GFC, dropping to $0.55
- April 2008 – Fone Zone changes name to Vita Group Limited – meaning 'way of life'
- 2009 – Vita Group consolidates multiple support locations into one central location
- March 2009 – Vita Group shares continue to feel impact of GFC, reaching a low of $0.06
- August 2009 – Vita Group signs licence agreement – allowing Vita to roll out 100 Telstra stores
- December 2009 – Market reacts well to Vita Group's licence agreement, with shares reaching $0.34
- 2010 – Vita Group's first Telstra Business Centre (TBC) opens
- September 2010 – Vita Group shares remain steady at $0.35
- 2011 – Vita Group launches Sprout accessory brand
- August 2012 – Vita Group sells Liquipel
- October 2012 – Vita Group opens its 85th Telstra store
- January 2013 – Vita Group share price is $0.46
- January 2013 – David McMahon leaves Vita Group
- January 2013 – Vita Group discontinues Liquipel
- August 2013 – Vita Group shares reach $0.78
- October 2013 – Vita Group acquires Camelon IT

- December 2014 – Vita Group's 100th Telstra store opens

- January 2015 – Investor confidence in Vita Group grows, with share price doubling in six months from $0.77 in July 2014 to $1.43 in January 2015

- January 2015 – Vita Group celebrates 20 years in retail

- January 2015 – Vita Group celebrates 20 years since first Fone Zone store

- August 2015 – Vita Group announces revenues of over $600 million

- January 2016 – Vita Group closes the Next Byte channel

- March 2016 – Telstra and Vita Group extend their relationship to 2020

- March 2016 – Vita Group shares hit $2.95

- May 2016 – Vita Group shares hit $4.21

Author's Note

In 2014 Maxine Horne approached me to help tell the story of her business and the lessons she had learnt riding the innovation wave created by the rise of the mobile phone and its convergence with digital technology. Like most people who meet Maxine, I was captured by her enthusiasm but, more importantly, by her candour in being willing to admit the mistakes she had made and the lessons she had learnt. That candour is central to this book, my third biography. Maxine has been generous with her time to help me meet tight deadlines and referred me to others important to her story and the story of the Vita Group.

This story is Maxine's and it has been my privilege to help bring it to life. In doing so, I have also drawn on my knowledge of business built over the past five years as

MC of the Australian Institute of Company Directors' Leaders' Edge lunches in Brisbane where I have publicly interviewed dozens of Australian and international CEOs. I have also referred to, or drawn on, a number of other texts which require acknowledgement. They include:

Australian Institute of Company Directors, course material, 2011

Erik Brynjolfsson and Andrew McAfee, *The Second Machine Age – Work, Progress, and Prosperity in a Time of Brilliant Technologies*, W.W. Norton & Co, 2014

Peter F. Drucker in the *Harvard Business Review*, Harvard University Press, 1991

Charles Duhigg, *The Power of Habit – Why We Do What We Do In Life and Business*, Random House, 2012

Hubbard, Samuel, Cocks and Heap, *The First XI – Winning Organisations In Australia*, John Wiley & Sons, 2007

Josh Linkner, *The Road to Reinvention – How to Drive Disruption and Accelerate Transformation*, Jossey Bass, 2014

Stephen C. Lundin, John Christensen and Harry Paul, *Fish! Sticks*, Hodder Mobius, 2003

Stephen C. Lundin, John Christensen and Harry Paul, *Fish! Tales*, Hodder Mobius, 2002

Madonna King